THE 10 WORST
OF EVERYTHING

THE 10 WORST OF EVERYTHING

THE BIG BOOK OF BAD

Sam Jordison

PORTABLE PRESS

San Diego, California

Portable Press
An imprint of Printers Row Publishing Group
10350 Barnes Canyon Road, Suite 100, San Diego, CA 92121
www.portablepress.com • mail@portablepress.com

Printers Row Publishing Group is a division of Readerlink Distribution Services, LLC. Portable Press is a registered trademark of Readerlink Distribution Services, LLC.

Correspondence regarding the content of this book should be sent to Portable Press, Editorial Department, at the above address. Author, illustration, and rights inquiries should be sent to Michael O'Mara Books Ltd.

Portable Press
Publisher: Peter Norton • Associate Publisher: Ana Parker
Senior Developmental Editor: April Graham Farr
Senior Product Manager: Kathryn C. Dalby
Production Team: Jonathan Lopes, Rusty von Dyl

Cover design: www.us-now.com

ISBN: 978-1-64517-160-7

Printed in China

23 22 21 20 19   1 2 3 4 5

To Elly and Polly

CONTENTS

INTRODUCTION

If you're old enough to remember back to 1997, you'll remember the popular refrain from the D:Ream song, telling us that "things can only get better." Back then, the idea didn't seem entirely ludicrous. Students still received free university education, the Cold War was receding in history's rearview mirror, Bill Clinton was president, and New Labour were about to take over in the UK. There was also a strong feeling that most of the twentieth century had been such a god-awful mess that it would be a big stretch for us to actually make things worse. But that was then: the happy days before Brexit and Trump. It turns out we did find ways to make things worse.

We usually do.

Humans have notched up some outstanding achievements over the ages, but the majority of us have always been more likely to mess up. For every Julius Caesar, there were thousands of Gauls running screaming into battle, semi-naked and doomed. For every John Lennon, there are millions of us who have never got further than singing badly into a mirror with a hairbrush microphone. Before the Wright brothers took to the sky, there were thousands of poor fools vainly flapping the wings they'd attached to their arms—and plummeting to earth . . .

1

Most books celebrate the exceptions rather than the rule. They focus on the overachievers, the unique and strange success stories. They don't provide a fair reflection of the general tide of history—but they do make your average reader feel, well, more average. *The 10 Worst of Everything* is here to redress this imbalance and show that you maybe shouldn't take it too badly if your own plans aren't working out. In fact, you're on the side of humanity. There's still more that we don't know than we do know. There's always more to put right. There's more to life than is dreamed of in most of our philosophies. And there's nearly always someone worse off than you. Which is reassuring.

It's also often amusing. And fascinating. Just as we can learn a lot from our own mistakes, there's plenty to be gleaned from all the other things that have gone wrong. And, given that there are so many of them, we're in luck.

True to this messy state of the world, the route *The 10 Worst of Everything* takes isn't always direct, and I've never feared taking a diversion if I've spotted something interesting along the way. I should also note, for the benefit of any determined literalists reading these words, that I haven't actually managed to squeeze **all** the bad things into this volume. I love a good list—but have assumed there are natural limits. My intention is for this book to provide a good compendium of facts about the world, some useful information about places to avoid, and various mind-boggling ideas about medicine, history, sport, food, culture, science, and all the ridiculous things we do to each other.

Of course, it's up for debate how we measure how bad something might be. Where there are useful statistics and recorded data, I've done my best to check and include them. I mention this research because I'm so keen to let you know I've done it. I'm not just making this crazy stuff up. And finding out the facts was often quite challenging. It hasn't always been easy to find reliable information about many of the subjects covered in these pages. But it has been all too easy to find unreliable information. I've previously written a book about fake news—but it turns out that there's almost as much false information about the kinds of things you might want to put into Top Tens on the internet as there is about Trump and Brexit. But no matter—the truth is out there and I hope I've been able to bring it to you. And where there are genuine authorities on the different topics I have done my best to acknowledge them.

Otherwise, it's pretty much me. By their nature, many of these lists are subjective and you are more than welcome to judge them accordingly. I say this not only to preempt anyone hoping to start making "worst book" jokes, but because I think part of the fun of any kind of chart is thinking about its faults. I hope you'll enjoy disagreeing with me as well as laughing along with me about the ridiculous plots of romantic comedy films, wincing at the sheer nasty power of crocodiles, and groaning about our leaders. Although I'm right about BMWs, as you'll see when you get to that part. I don't think there should be any argument there . . .

CHAPTER 1

BAD NATURE

Throughout history, we humans have got an awful lot wrong. On the plus side, we have at least managed to survive this far. Which is no mean feat—especially given how much of creation appears to be arrayed against us.

THE TEN SCARIEST HUMAN PARASITES*

Parasites can most simply be defined as organisms that derive nutrients at another organism's expense. Total capitalist bastards, in other words.

10. Tapeworm

Huge long worms that live in your gut, grow several feet in length, shed segments of themselves, lay eggs inside you and—ugh! ugh!—form cysts that migrate around you, hoping you will die and rot in the street so they can move on to infect whatever other animals eat you.

9. Scabies mite

These little bandits burrow into your skin and defecate in your blood, producing unbearable itching. If you're especially

~~~~~~~~~~~~~~~~~~~~~~

*Depending on how you look at things, you may think that parasites that don't affect humans can be even worse. There's one that bites the tongues off red snappers—then continues to live in the poor fish's mouth, drinking its blood and attaching itself to its tongue muscles. The parasite then takes up permanent residence, flapping around, in horrible imitation of the organ it's destroyed. There's also a wasp that injects venom into a cockroach's brain, hypnotizes it to carry it back to its burrow, snacks on half of it, lays its eggs inside the remains and leaves them to finally finish off the corpse when they turn into cocoons. Oh, and there's a really weird thing that lives in poo before getting eaten by snails—at which point it goes to the snail's eyestalks, turns them into green things that look like caterpillars, while also taking over the snail's brain, giving it new warped stalks that are perpetually on show so that birds come and eat them . . . thus allowing the parasite to lay eggs inside the bird . . . which are then shat out to begin the whole horrible cycle again. This parasite is called *Leucocloridium paradoxum*, which is Latin for "f★ck off and don't come near me!"

lucky, they'll bring along millions of their friends with them and give you crusted scabies—which is every bit as awful as it sounds.

8. Screwworm fly

The Latin for screwworm fly is *Cochliomyia hominivorax*. *Cochliomyia* means "twisted worm"—a pretty direct alternative for the English term "screwworm." *Hominivorax* means "man-eating." And that's because this delinquent creature lays maggots inside open wounds which then burrow into your flesh with special cutting jaws. If you try to remove them, they burrow deeper, troughing their way through muscles, blood vessels, and sometimes vital organs.

7. Australian paralysis tick

It gets worse. Not only do these unspeakable little terrorists lend you all their diseases when they drink your blood, they secrete a toxin that causes paralysis and, in some cases, stops your lungs from working.

6. Ascaris

This is a fairly common worm infection. But just because ascaris worms infest lots of bodies that doesn't make them any less foul. They're bad enough when they're gushing out of your rear like great clumps of nightmare spaghetti. But they can also get to your lungs. And in that case, they sometimes start to crawl out of your mouth and nose. Which is pretty much the worst thing that can happen to you on a date—aside from hearing your love interest declaring they voted for Donald Trump.

5. Filarial worm

These roundworms clog lymphatic vessels, preventing fluid from draining properly and causing the huge painful swelling and tissue deformity known as elephantiasis. Thanks for that.

4. Guinea worm

Guinea worms start off in water fleas. Once inside the stomach of anyone unlucky enough to drink the infected water, the fleas dissolve and the worms burst out into the body. They burrow into the intestinal wall. They grow over 3 feet long. And if a female finds a mate, she can produce 3 million embryos.[*] At which point she slithers painfully through subcutaneous tissue to the foot, causing an agonizing, burning blister. When this develops, the victim can't help but plunge the painful place in water—at which point the worm vomits out her 3 million babies, ready to infect more fleas. Her unwilling host next has to spend weeks rolling her out around a stick, all the time praying she doesn't snap and cause further infection.

3. *Naegleria fowleri*

Oh sh*t! This is an amoeba that eats brains. Anyone unlucky enough to ingest infected water through the nose can develop

*Three million. Oh hell no. I'm never leaving the house again.

primary amoebic meningoencephalitis (PAM). Symptoms start with headaches, move on to hallucinations and seizures, and end, after two horrible weeks, in death in almost 95 percent of cases.

2. *Onchocerca volvulus*

These wormy parasites spread throughout the body and cause intense itching when they die. They can also provoke an immune reaction, which can in turn cause a condition known as river blindness—the world's second greatest cause of infectious blindness. They may well be the single most persuasive proof that there is no beneficent god.

1. Plasmodium

Malaria is the result of infection by this parasitic protozoan. The little murderer is responsible for millions of fatalities every year.

THE TEN DEADLIEST INSECTS

Sure, yes, the circle of life. The beautiful complexity of our ecosystem. The way every little piece of the puzzle contributes to the rest. I'm not saying insects aren't useful. But even at the best of times, they're annoying. Meanwhile, at the worst . . . Well, here we go …

10. Botfly

These get extra points for being disgusting. Their larvae burrow into flesh and the gut with agonizing results. Trying to squeeze them out can cause their bodies to rupture, and their bodily fluids can then cause fatal anaphylactic shocks.

9. Triatominae

Also known as kissing bugs, these little blighters suck your blood and come preloaded with nasty diseases. They particularly favor passing on Chagas disease, which slowly rots your intestines and destroys your heart.

8. Fire ants

Yes, they are called fire ants because their bite burns. A single bite is a horribly painful experience and can cause wounds that swell and rupture alarmingly. But the real trouble comes because these nightmare creatures tend to swarm and thousands can attack you all at once. They kill 150 people a day worldwide and destroy crops almost as efficiently as locusts.

7. Japanese hornets

Like giant wasps on steroids—and with all the accompanying rage issues. They can hit you repeatedly with a sting that has more acetylcholine[*] than any other stinging insect, and which also contains an enzyme that can dissolve human tissue. Oh, and a chemical that encourages other hornets to start attacking you. They kill dozens of people every year. And if they go for you, they'll make you wish you'd never been born. Japanese hornets are also notorious for taking on and destroying entire hives of honey bees with only a handful of their malevolent, pumped-up buddies to help them.

6. Killer bees

But bees aren't just innocent victims in all of this. Africanized honey bees are brutal. They can follow their victims for up to a mile, stinging their eyes and face, sometimes in swarms of up to 80,000 members.

5. Bullet ants

As well as causing an extremely painful wound, a bullet ant sting can also block blood flow. Better still, they attack without warning, dropping onto their luckless victims from the trees above them.

---

*That's the stuff that hurts.

4. Driver ants

Also known as Dorylus, these ants from central and east Africa march in columns of up to 50 million insects. A column can travel at 21 yards an hour. And if you get stuck in the way of that column, it will devour you. The ant's jaws don't let go even if you snap the rest of their bodies in half. They have even been known to eat elephants. Most terrifying, though, is the fact that they have been known to march into houses at night, while people inside are sleeping …

3. Tsetse flies

They carry sleeping sickness, kill around 300,000 people a year, and have rendered great swathes of Africa uninhabitable. The little sh*ts.

2. Locusts

Again, locusts don't seem like much of a direct threat, individually. But if you've got a plague of these beasts eating your crops you're going to take them seriously—or starve. Locusts still destroy thousands of acres of crops every year.

1. Anopheles mosquitoes

An individual mosquito bite may be more annoying than painful, but thanks to their tendency to carry plasmodium and so cause blood-borne diseases like malaria, Anopheles mosquitoes are responsible for more deaths annually than all other insects combined. They can f*ck right off.

THE TEN DEADLIEST SCORPIONS

Scorpions sting around 500,000 people every year in Mexico alone—and 150,000 of those people require antivenom. However, they rarely kill. Scorpions also often live in deserts and many species have had little contact with humans. There are considerable knowledge gaps about these little warriors, and there could even be a real badass out there that no one has encountered yet. As a result, this list is rather patchy. Thanks to a confusing taxonomy system when it comes to scorpions, it's also been impossible to provide ten discrete entries. The anal-retentive part of me has been itching to dis-include them. But another part just says: scorpions! They're hardcore. They have to feature.

10–4. Androctonus varieties

Also known as the fat-tail scorpion,[*] the androctonus[†] produces the most potent of all scorpion venom with symptoms including seizures, unconsciousness, and hypertension. It is also extremely aggressive. The good news is that there is a widely available antivenom and it takes several hours before the poison really does damage. The bad news is that there are about twenty varieties of this bad boy and most of them can mess you up— which is why I've allowed them to take over so much of this list.[‡]

---

[*]So called because they have a fat tail. Not everything has to be difficult.

[†]So called because they kill men. *Andros* is Greek for man, *ctonus* comes from *kteinein*, the verb to kill. That one was a bit harder.

[‡]Strictly speaking I should have had twenty different entries labeled "4=," and I guess I could have tried to explain the minute differences between the various fat-tails. But hey. Bite me. (Just don't sting me.)

3. Brazilian yellow scorpion

This scorpion stings thousands in Brazil every year. This sting is extremely painful and often causes nausea and an alarming increase in heart rate. Sometimes it also causes hyperesthesia—meaning its victims become extremely and painfully sensitive to anything that touches their skin. In the elderly and very young it can also cause respiratory failure.

2. Deathstalker scorpion

It's only about 2.5 in. long, but as well as having a name like the ultimate Marvel villain, this scorpion can inject you with a cocktail of toxins that attack your heart and nervous system. It rarely kills healthy adults—unless they are unlucky enough to have an additional allergic reaction to the bite. But it does kill children and leaves many who survive its attentions with pancreatitis. (On the plus side, its venom has been used in cancer research and scientists think it has the potential to treat diabetes too. Swings and roundabouts.)

1. Indian red scorpion

Clinical studies of bites from these little extremists have reported fatality rates between 8 and 40 percent, placing them among the most dangerous creatures on earth. Symptoms include vomiting, priapism,* dizziness, heart flutters, shock,

*Endless erections—but not in a good way.

inflammation of the heart, and respiratory failure. The species is native to India and can also be found in Pakistan, Nepal, and Sri Lanka. In all these places, you are advised to check your shoes before you put them on.

THE TEN DEADLIEST SPIDERS

Spiders may look terrifying, but they aren't as dangerous as is often supposed. Few tend to use the venom in their bite when defending themselves against humans—and even then, the bites are rarely fatal. Statistically, it's more likely that you'll be struck by lightning than bitten by a spider. Meanwhile, humans are almost 75,000 times more likely to kill you. (Which is only sort-of reassuring, I know.)

10. Tarantula

I remember vividly being told in the school playground that tarantulas are the most poisonous things on earth. But apparently not everything you hear in the playground is true.* If severely provoked, South American tarantulas produce painful bites, but their venom is weak. Some Asian species like tiger spiders are more aggressive and their bites have resulted in hospitalization. But they are not known to be fatal.

9. Redback

A close relative of the black widow (see page 18), these spiders can cause painful bites, muscle weakness, and vomiting. In April 2016, an Australian construction worker encountered a redback in a portable toilet—and the very worst thing happened. The man

---

*While I'm dealing with playground myths, crane flies are not poisonous. And no, I don't think you can get pregnant from swimming pool water.

(whom the media named only as "Jordan") went through several hours of agony and terror before he was discharged from hospital. Five months later, he visited another Portaloo, and yes, another one bit his todger. "I'm the most unlucky guy in the country at the moment," he ruefully told the BBC.

8. Brown widow spider

The venom of the brown widow is actually more toxic than that of their relative, the black widow. Luckily, they don't inject as much of it when they bite. Mind you, they can still hurt. Those who have enjoyed their attentions have compared the experience to being hit with a sledgehammer.

7. Mouse spider

These spiders are fat and furry and supposedly have mouse-like features: if you can imagine a mouse with eight legs and venomous fangs. An encounter with these latter can cause muscle spasms, nausea, and severe ouchy-ouchy.

6. Chilean and brown recluse spider

Bites from these spiders can cause kidney failure and produce wounds that sometimes go gangrenous. Fortunately, as their name suggests, they do as much as they can to avoid humans.

5. Six-eyed sand spider

There's no known antivenom and the bite of the six-eyed sand spider is toxic to cells. It can destroy tissues and organs, as well as causing blood clots, lesions, bleeding from the skin and orifices, and eventually, death. That's the bad news. The good news is that there are no proven cases of these spiders biting anyone.

4. Black widow spider

As well as having the coolest name of all spiders, black widows look good. Not only are they sleek, black, and shiny, but they have fierce red marks on their back. These are either shaped like two triangles point to point, or they look eerily like an hourglass . . . And yes, this timing device is going to start to feel all too relevant if a black widow bites you. Their venom causes latrodectism—which is to say, spasming and paralysis. It's alarming stuff, but since the development of antivenoms, very few humans have died because of black widows. (Unlike the poor old male of the species, which gets eaten immediately after copulation.)

3. Brazilian wandering spider

This spider sometimes tops most-deadly lists because of the toxicity of its venom. But it rarely actually uses that venom when it bites. Only around 1 percent of encounters with Brazilian wandering spiders get serious—and even then only children are considered to be at real risk of death.

2. Northern tree funnel web

This spider hangs out in trees in the north of Australia rather than gardens in Sydney. Otherwise, it's a pretty similar deal to the Sydney funnel web. Which you can read about right here …

1. Sydney funnel web

The relative dangers presented by different spider species are a matter of debate—but Guinness World Records have decided Sydney funnel webs are the most dangerous and I'm not about to argue. This spider gets its name because—guess what?—it lives in Sydney (generally within 43.5 miles of the center of the city—and often in people's gardens) and its web is, yes, funnel shaped (it generally builds them inside holes or crevices). It doesn't have the most potent venom of all species, but the funnel web often bites its victims several times and its poison is fast acting. Dr. Robert Raven of the Queensland Museum told *The Guardian*: "In terms of speed of death, in Australia we say funnel web, 15 minutes, no sweat."

THE TEN MOST VENOMOUS SNAKES

This list is measured in numbers of mice that can be killed by just one dose of venom delivered by the snake in question.[*] Some snake species, such as Belcher's sea snake, have more potent venom than those listed here, but don't deliver enough of it in one bite to be as harmful. It's also worth noting that some of the snakes on this list—such as the taipan—are not particularly aggressive. It's possible to argue that some species of mambas are more dangerous. But at the point of contact, these are the snakes that are most likely to kill you.

Meanwhile, on the subject of arguing, when it comes to snakes versus scorpions versus spiders versus insects, snakes win. They do far more damage worldwide, bite millions of people every year and kill thousands. They are responsible for almost 50,000 deaths annually in India alone.

10. Terciopelo

163,113 mice

9. Central African gaboon viper

166,667 mice

8. Forest cobra

170,062 mice

---

*The data was taken from snakedatabase.org on May 4, 2018. I'm guessing they use mice thanks to an unsurprising lack of human volunteers.

7. Indian krait
187,500 mice

6. Monocled cobra
250,676 mice

5. Mozambique spitting cobra
395,181 mice

4. Inland taipan
482,222 mice

3. Indian cobra
554,545 mice

2. Mainland tiger snake
636,000 mice

1. Coastal taipan
4,900,000 mice

THE TEN DEADLIEST HUNTERS IN NATURE

On the one hand, Mother Nature cradles us all in her luscious, fragrant, life-giving embrace. On the other, she kicks ass.

10. Wolf

Pound for pound, it's hard to beat wolves. A pack hunting together can take on animals far in excess of their own individual sizes. They're also smart and cooperate in complicated relays to ensure that they remain fresher than whatever poor dumb creature they're running down. Meanwhile, they have over 200 million scent cells (humans have fewer than 5 million) and can sniff out prey more than 1 mile away. They can also hear sounds up to 6 miles away. Oh, and one wolf can eat almost 22 pounds of meat in one sitting (around 100 burgers).

9. Army ants

A colony of ants can take out 30,000 insects and small animals in a day. This feat seems slightly less impressive when you know that a colony can contain up to half a million ants—but I'd still be running rather than counting.

8. Harbor porpoise

Sure, they look like mini versions of Flipper the dolphin, but these porpoises aren't half so cute from the point of view of the fish they eat. Using a sophisticated system of echolocation calls (think: dolphin sonar), they are able to round up and catch 90 percent of the prey they hunt. Which makes them among the most effective hunters out there. That's why they are able to get through an impressive 550 fish an hour—or 3,000 a day.

7. Dragonfly

A 2012 study at Harvard[*] found that dragonflies are even more effective hunters than porpoises and can catch and kill 95 percent of the things they chase. It's a good job they're so small.

6. Cheetah

Unlike dragonflies, cheetahs only manage to catch the prey they target about 50 percent of the time. But they can reach speeds of almost 60 mph and they have massive sharp teeth and claws. You try outrunning one.

5. Blue whale

Okay. They aren't known for attacking big impressive prey. But if you're a krill, blue whales are going to really mess up your sh*t. And not just you. They will get through 40 million of your little crustacean buddies each and every day.

4. Tiger

It isn't their size or their beauty, their speed or their massive jaws. All those things are impressive enough, but to get the real measure of how hardcore tigers are, you have to pay attention to

---

*You can find it here: http://jeb.biologists.org/content/215/6/903.
Dragonflies are impressive. Muscles in their wings allow incredible acceleration and maneuverability. Their eyes are also crazily complex and well adapted to spotting movement against the sky.

the creatures around them. When tigers appear on the scene, every other animal goes completely silent. Birds stop singing. Pigs stop truffling. Bears hold still. No one wants to piss off a tiger. On land, they are the ultimate boss.

3. Saltwater crocodile

A saltwater crocodile jaw can exert a force of 3,700 pounds per square inch. That's more powerful than any other bite on earth. And while they're crushing your head as if it's a ripe tomato, they also roll you underwater and drown you for good measure.

2. Great white shark

Great whites can grow to more than 19 feet long. They can weigh almost 2 tons. They have 300 serrated teeth. They often chase down prey from as far as 0.6 miles away—and they detect that luckless living meat thanks to the electromagnetic pulses given off from its movements. Including the beating of its heart. So staying still won't help you. Nor will swimming, since Great whites can move through the water at 25 mph.

1. Killer whales

Killer whales can weigh more than 6.5 tons and eat great white sharks. *QED.*[*]

***

*They also kill dolphins by throwing them out of the water and breaking their spines. Nasty!

NATURE'S DEADLIEST PLANTS

Killer whales might be very good at throwing their weight around, but some of nature's most effective killers are lighter than feathers and don't even have to move to destroy you.

10. Oleander

Oleander[*] is a purple flower grown all over the southern USA as a decorative shrub. But it's not so pretty once it gets inside you, since it's rich in cardiac glycosides with troubling names like oleandrin, folinerin, and digitoxigenin. These can cause increased heart rate and sudden death. The plant also messes with your stomach and makes you both puke and poop uncontrollably.

9. White snakeroot

This plant contains tremetol, a type of alcohol that causes tremors, vomiting, delirium, and death. Cows like to munch on it—which is a worry because eating the flesh or drinking the milk of an animal that's ingested the plant can lead to severe illness. Legend has it that it was this "milk sickness" that killed Abraham Lincoln's mother.

---

*There's an internet rumor that the Italian translation of the plant's name is "ass kicker." Alas, this isn't true. It's just called *oleandro* in Italy—which has no extra meaning. But still, you can see where the idea came from.

8. Manchineel

Also known as *manzanilla de la muerte*—little apple of death—this is a singularly unfriendly tree. If you brush against it, it causes a blistering allergic reaction on your skin. If you persist in approaching and eat its fruit, you'll ingest a healthy dose of physostigmine. An overdose of this can induce vomiting, nausea, stomach pain, dyspepsia, diarrhea, and seizures.

7. Suicide tree

Guess why this one got its name? The seeds of this Indian tree contain cerberin, a powerful toxin that disrupts ion channels in the heart and can be fatal in sufficient quantities. A report by the Laboratory of Analytical Toxicology in La Voulte-sur-Rhône, France, listed more than 500 cases of *Cerbera* poisoning between 1989 and 1999 in the south-west Indian state of Kerala alone and suggested that there could have been twice as many that weren't recorded.

6. Deadly nightshade

Closely related to the potato and tomato, this vegetable of death is loaded up with a poison called solanine, as well as a good dose of atropine, scopolamine, and hyoscyamine. If you munch its berries you will experience hallucinations, blurred vision, and a painfully dry mouth. Your behavior may turn aggressive. Your heart will beat so loud it becomes audible several feet away. Then you will enter a coma. And possibly die. Deadly nightshade's taxonomical name is *Atropa belladonna*. *Atropa* after the Greek goddess Atropos who cut the threads of life. *Belladonna* meaning "beautiful woman"—because ladies in the seventeenth century used to put extract of deadly nightshade in their eyes to dilate their pupils. This is not recommended.

5. Lily of the valley

With its white bell flowers, the lily of the valley looks lovely, but it contains no fewer than 38 chemicals that will mess with your heart rate. It also causes stomach pain, drowsiness, rashes, vomiting, and for that special extra touch, excessive urination.

4. Hemlock

Hemlock was used to kill Socrates in 399 BC. Plato described a peaceful death for his philosophical mentor, but actually coniine, the main poison in the plant, provides an agonizing end. It causes an ascending muscular paralysis, beginning in the legs and working upward to the respiratory muscles and so, a slow painful expiration.[*]

*The Ancient Greeks were well aware of the nature of death by hemlock. Plato wasn't fooling anyone. Nicander of Colophon in 204 BC wrote that it made its victim's eyes roll, caused men to crawl on their hands and then: "a terrible choking blocks the lower throat and . . . windpipe; the extremities grow cold . . . the victim draws breath like one swooning, and his spirit beholds Hades."

3. Aconite

Also known as monk's hood (because of its cowl-like shape), wolfsbane (because shepherds used it to tip their arrows when hunting wolves), and devil's helmet (because of course Old Nick would wear a very poisonous hat). This flower is very beautiful and grows widely in mountains throughout Europe and Asia. Just touching it can cause nausea and stomach cramps. Eating it, meanwhile, causes a burning in the mouth, vomiting, diarrhea, drooling—and then the fun really begins, with victims experiencing tingling, numbness, heart flutters, and then death, thanks to respiratory failure.

2. Castor beans

Castor oil plants are found in gardens all over the world—and castor oil was once a popular medicinal purgative. But the seeds also contain a chemical called ricin, which is so toxic that Guinness World Records lists it as the most poisonous plant in the world. It takes four to eight seeds to kill you—and if you eat those, you'll have an agonizing three to five days of abdominal pain, bloody flux, and burning sensations in your mouth and throat.

1. Tobacco

Every part of the plant is toxic and, unlike the other items on this list, it actually kills millions of people every year. So put that in your pipe and smoke it. (Actually, don't.)

THE MOST DANGEROUS MUSHROOMS

If anyone ever offers to cook you a meal from mushrooms they've foraged, just say no. Order a pizza.

10. Fool's funnel

No, this is not another name for Boris Johnson's mouth. It's a mushroom that causes muscarine poisoning: excessive salivation, sweating, sickness, and respiratory problems. It's rarely fatal for healthy adults, but still brings plenty of pain.

9. Angel wing

A delicate spreading mushroom that looks like angel wings—and, yes, speeds you on to meeting the airy trumpeters. The mushroom isn't yet well understood, but is known to cause problems in the brain and liver. In 2004, it killed seventeen people in Japan in six weeks. Some people still classify it as food. This seems unwise.

8. Deadly dapperling

Does what it says on the tin. A small mushroom packed with amatoxin, a deadly poison that attacks the liver.

7. *Podostroma cornu-damae*

This vivid red fungus sprouts in finger-like tubes, rising from the earth like the hands of the damned. It contains trichothecene mycotoxins, which cause hair loss, peeling skin, and liver failure, among other unappealing symptoms. It has caused a number of deaths in Japan and Korea.

6. *Conocybe filaris*

These ones look like hallucinogenic magic mushrooms—and as a result have killed almost as many hippies as President Nixon. Like many other species on this list they contain amatoxin.

5. Deadly webcap

Deadly webcaps contain orellanine, a mycotoxin that causes hallucinations and renal failure. These little sneaks also look dangerously like other edible mushroom species. They've lured plenty of people into making a big mistake as a result—among them, the author of *The Horse Whisperer*, Nicholas Evans. He, his wife, and two guests ate some in 2008. They survived—but suffered kidney failure. They were luckier than a gathering of 135 people in Poland who accidentally consumed orellanine in 1957. Nineteen of them died and many others had suffered lifelong problems.

4. Autumn skullcap

Like many other fatal mushrooms, the skullcap bears a close resemblance to edible mushrooms (this time honey fungus). Again it contains amatoxin and will kill you.

3. False morel

Confusingly, this fungus doesn't look anything like a morel. It actually looks like a brain. So naturally, people love to eat it—especially in Scandinavia and eastern Europe. The trouble is that if it isn't cooked properly it passes on a toxin that turns into monomethylhydrazine inside the body. Which is bad news because monomethylhydrazine attacks the nervous system and can wipe out your kidneys.

2. Destroying angel

Mushrooms don't mess around when it comes to names, do they? This little menace is loaded with amatoxin and bad news.

1. Death cap

Death caps look like the edible species paddy straw mushrooms. They are also reported to taste nice. But this mushroom packs so much amatoxin that, soon after eating it, people start gushing from both ends with vomit and diarrhea. Cruelly, the patients then begin to feel fine, but the toxins in the mushroom continue to quietly ravage their liver. Then, after a few days: death.

THE TEN STUPIDEST ANIMALS

Natural selection has produced some marvels. But quite a few subpar specimens have also managed to survive far longer than they ought. If Charles Darwin had only studied these species instead of all the marvelous creatures he encountered on the voyage of *The Beagle*, we might still be stuck thinking that the earth was created in seven days …

10. Woodpeckers

They make their nests and call for mates by smashing their heads into trees. You probably wouldn't want a woodpecker on your bar's trivia team.

9. Banana slugs

These slugs are hermaphrodites. When they start out, they all have penises that emerge from genital pores on their heads. When they mate, they curl up together and penetrate each other at the same time. Which all sounds reasonable enough, if you're into that kind of thing and don't mind being a literal d*ckhead. But the next bit is weird. Banana slugs engage in apophallation: which is to say, one slug bites off the other's penis. The theory is that it's to reduce competition for their own sperm. Which also makes sense. Except it turns out that most of the time the slug who's had its knob eaten gets annoyed and responds by chomping on its erstwhile mate's junk in turn. Be grateful that you aren't a banana slug.

8. Cane toads

Banana slugs' mating habits are at least smarter than male cane toads. These ugly brutes will try to hump anything—and spend hours in the attempt. They have even been observed expending colossal energy on female cane toads that have been run over by cars.

7. Turkeys

Depressingly, chickens are more intelligent than you might imagine. They can even count. Luckily, there are no such worries about turkeys. They might not drown in the rain[*] as per popular myth, but otherwise there's plenty of silly to celebrate here. This, after all, is a creature for which "gobble-gobble" represents the pinnacle of intellectual conversation. Turkeys also suffer from tetanic torticollar spasms. Meaning that, every so often, they will freeze and stare at the sky for more than half a minute without blinking. Since we've broached the uncomfortable subject of weird mating, you should perhaps know that male turkeys will try to mate with anything with a turkey head. Including clay models of turkeys. And worse still, dead turkey heads that have been severed from turkey bodies.

*While we're myth busting: no, ostriches do not bury their heads in the sand to hide from prey. They do it to forage for stones and grit that help their digestion.

6. Sponges

They often look like brains, but they don't have them.* Go figure.

5. Koalas

Koalas have unusually small cerebra for mammals, but the stupid doesn't end there. They live exclusively on eucalyptus, which is so hard to digest that they have had to develop four stomachs to cope.

4. Dodos

Yes, killing dodos was an all-too-telling demonstration of man's horrible ability to wreak havoc in the natural world. Recent zoological studies have tried to prove that dodos' brains were more capable than is popularly supposed, since they were relatively quite big. But then again, these were plump, slow, flightless birds. Of course the hungry sailors who found them on Mauritius couldn't resist eating them. Not least because, dumbest of all, dodos had no fear of humans.

3. Kakapos

This flightless New Zealand bird has a lot in common with the dodo. It wanders around on the jungle floor and humans have ruined its once peaceful existence. Before we came along, the

*Sponges lack tissues and organs, but they are multicellular, don't have plant-style cell walls, and produce sperm. So they are classed as animals.

kakapo had no natural predators. So unused are they to being attacked that they either freeze when something goes for them, or climb a tree. And if you're thinking that that second action seems reasonable, think again. Because once they've got up onto a reasonably elevated branch, kakapos jump off, forgetting that they can't fly. Meaning that they tend to serve themselves up in a broken heap at their assailant's feet.

2. Giant pandas

They might look adorable, but giant pandas are really a huge cuddly evolutionary mistake. They only eat bamboo, which is so low in nutrients that they have to munch at the stuff all the waking day. Leaving them no space for anything else. They are particularly bad at mating. And if they ever do successfully copulate, the females often don't realize they're pregnant, freak out when the cubs emerge, and kill them. Or just roll over them in their sleep and crush them. It's as if they want to die out.

1. Humans

Sure, yes, space travel, yes, Proust, yes, Shakespeare, yes, those corkscrews that open bottles with special levers so you don't even have to twist anything. But against all our successes you also have to weigh Katie Hopkins, Piers Morgan, and the guy at your school who always set light to the gas pipes in chemistry lessons.

CHAPTER 2

COMMUNICATION BREAKDOWNS

"Sticks and stones may break my bones, but words will never hurt me." Whoever invented that rhyme had obviously never tried to speak Welsh or lift an unabridged version of *In Search of Lost Time*. Let alone faced the sharp end of a Shakespearean insult. Language and literature contain many of humanity's greatest achievements, but, by the same token, they also give us the words to explain our failings.

THE TEN HARDEST LANGUAGES FOR ENGLISH SPEAKERS TO LEARN

It should be noted that English itself is no walk in the park, with hundreds of irregular verbs, a huge vocabulary, exceptions to just about every grammatical rule, a non-phonetic spelling system, endless homophones, many bizarre ways of ordering words and adding emphasis, at least eight grammatical ways to talk about the future, and weird assholes like Donald Trump mangling the language on Twitter every day. But since you're reading this book, I'm assuming you've got most of the basics. You might find these languages more challenging.

10. Arabic

It boasts an unusual script that runs from right to left, with letters written in four different forms depending on where they're placed in a word. Working out what the hell is going on is made still more difficult because there are no vowels in the written form of the language.

9. Mongolian

Thankfully, the old Mongolian writing system, which used to run up and down the page, has been transposed into the more comprehensible Cyrillic since 1941. But learning Mongolian still presents some brutal tests for the uninitiate. It is, for instance, a language which relies on "vowel harmony." Meaning, vowels are classified according to where in your mouth you sound them. Which might be okay, if there wasn't also a rule that vowels from different groups can't be used in the same word. And if the way you pronounced those words didn't entirely alter their meaning.

8. Korean

Korean is a language isolate: it doesn't fit in with any other language family. It consequently has a unique and difficult vocabulary, not to mention sentence structures that baffle English speakers, since the verb tends to come last. (So Koreans say, "I like a crazy man drive" rather than "I drive like a crazy man.") Oh, and there are seven levels of formality for social situations, each with different verb endings.

7. Georgian

Here is the Georgian for "your mother": შენი დედამოწყან. And while there's definitely some appeal to being rude in an alphabet that has letters that look like bosoms (თ), sperm (დ), and a person on a space-hopper (ჰ), there are considerable obstacles to overcome. The language has two different "p" sounds, for instance. Most outsiders can't differentiate between them.* There's also an extensive case system, as well as nouns that don't follow the usual pattern of English when it comes to the subject and object of the verb, which tend to contain great clusters of consonants. Ouch.

---

*We can get technical down here in the footnote. Georgian is full of "glottalized plosives"—which is to say, hard-sounding consonants that vary in meaning depending on where in the larynx you produce the sound that makes them. It hurts to think about this, let alone try to make the correct noise variations.

6. Polish

There are seventeen different words for seven. And all other numerals. There are seven different noun cases, each one with variant genders. They have an extra range of sibilants ("ś" and "ć" as well as "s" and "c," for instance) and words are loaded down with "w"s and "z"s. Wrap your brain around this: *Na wyścigu wyścigowym wyścigówka wyścigowa wyścignęła wyścigówkę wyścigową numer sześć.**

5. Mandarin Chinese

Chinese is a tonal language. Which is to say, the meaning of a word changes depending on the tone with which it's pronounced. Therefore, many of the "same" words mean different things. Which becomes even more confusing thanks to the thousands of characters in the writing system. And the fact that verbs lack tenses. And the fact that the language has been around for thousands of years and can more than rival English for odd idioms, confusing aphorisms, and baffling expressions.

4. Cantonese Chinese

It's like Mandarin—only totally, bewilderingly different. It relies on many of the same tonal principles and has a similar basic alphabet, but then it's as if all those characters have been thrown in the air and arranged in crazily new patterns.

---

*That's Polish for, "The race-racing racetrack racing racer raced racecar number six." They have the best tongue twisters.

3. Japanese

Japanese has three different writing systems and thousands of characters in each alphabet. You're in for hours of hard yakka even before you even begin learning the hugely complicated vocabulary and grammar.

2. Hungarian

Hungarian is another near-isolate language, so the vocabulary is unlike any other on earth. The meaning of words can also be changed by suffixes that act in a variety of complex grammatical ways. Nouns consequently have eighteen different cases. Verbs, meanwhile, can be conjugated in five different forms.[*] Which is hard to explain, let alone write. On the plus side, Hungarian is brilliant for swearing. One common expression is *Nyald ki a seggem!*, which means: "Lick my ass out."[†]

1. Finnish

Finnish has fewer cases than Hungarian (just fifteen!), but also comes equipped with special additional complications. One clever trick the language pulls is to present single and double letter combinations with minutely different sounds, but hugely different meanings. *Tuli* and *Tuuli* mean "fire" and "wind," respectively. And look here: *Talotta* means "without a house." But *talolta* means "from a house." Meanwhile, words tend to

---

[*]According to tense, mood, person, definiteness, and number.
[†]There is also the excellent *menj a halál faszara!*, an instruction to "go onto Death's dick!"

41

get stuck together in huge compounds—and all those words come from a vocabulary system completely alien to English. Fortunately, Finnish is also excellent for swearing. *A'paskaa syövä koiranraiskaaja*, for instance, is a "sh*t eating dog rapist." So now you know.[*]

---

[*]And what could be more Finnish than *suksi vittuun*, the request that your interlocutor skis into a vagina?

THE TEN MOST EGREGIOUS EXAMPLES OF RIDICULOUS MANAGEMENT SPEAK

You can learn a lot about humanity by looking at the quality of its leaders. From whom you can learn just about nothing useful …

10. Going forward

"Going forward" is often used by bosses as a synonym for "that's enough from you, shut up, we're doing it my way"—and to strike fear into other workers. Otherwise, it's just a typical complification of perfectly serviceable language. What was wrong with "from now on" or "in future"?

9. Product evangelist

Like a salesperson, only with an extra icky weird edge.

8. Benchmarking

"Measuring," only with a crappy redundant metaphor thrown in. Originally, a benchmark was a surveyor's mark, cut into a wall or pillar, used as a reference point to measure height. Now it just shows how low language can be made to go.

7. Coterminosity

If something is coterminous, it has the same boundaries in space, or time, as something else. But even with this information, I still don't properly know (or care) what this overused buzzword means.

6. Action and actionables

Action and actionables are needless extra words to describe things you can do. For instance, you can action telling anyone who talks to you about actionables to action sticking them in their most-actionables.

5. Deliverables

A deliverable is an actionable that you can provide to someone. Which is to say, an extra word for an extra word you don't need or want anyway.

4. Low-hanging fruit

Management loves people to gather low-hanging fruit. It's a term used to describe things that can be easily "actioned." But also, disturbingly, a bulldog's bollocks.

3. Drill down

Can we drill down into just why this phrase has become so omnipresent? Is it because it's a kind of phallic version of "find out" with its suggestion of power tools and thrusting? Does that make you feel all unpleasanted-upon too?

2. Thought leader

Thought leaders are inevitably people with radio microphones who can neither think nor lead. At the time of writing, there are more than 87,000 people who have described themselves as thought leaders on Linkedin.com. Which begs the question: where are all the thought followers?

1. Sunset

Another gloopy euphemism. If you're going to "sunset" something, what you're actually going to do is to put it out of action. Or fire it. At best, you are going to stop doing it. Let's just sunset the whole thing shall we?

THE TEN MOST BRUTAL SHAKESPEAREAN INSULTS

Turns out that the Bard didn't just compare people to summer's days. He had plenty more up his puffy sleeve. Not all of it quite so complimentary.

10. *"A most notable coward, an infinite and endless liar, an hourly promise breaker, the owner of no one good quality."*

Parolles doesn't get a favorable introduction in *All's Well That Ends Well.*

9. *"Thou sodden-witted lord! thou hast no more brain than I have in mine elbows; an assinego may tutor thee: thou scurvy-valiant ass."*

Theristes lashes Ajax in *Troilus and Cressida.* "Sodden-witted" means "drunk-witted." An "assinego" is a very stupid person. Theristes is saying Ajax knows less than the biggest dumb ass around. Oh, and assinego also means "little ass"—hence the ass joke in the line that follows. A "scurvy-valiant ass" is just your standard disease-ridden donkey. Good old Shakespeare.

8. *"Bloody, bawdy villain! Remorseless, treacherous, lecherous, kindless villain!"*

Hamlet doesn't like his sex-hungry Uncle Claudius.

7. *"As fat as butter"*

A cruel description of Falstaff in *Henry IV Part 1*[*]

6. *"You starveling, you eel-skin, you dried neat's-tongue, you bull's-pizzle, you stock-fish! O, for breath to utter what is like thee! You tailor's-yard, you sheath, you bow-case, you vile standing tuck!"*

Falstaff got some insults of his own in too. He directed this foul-mouthed tirade at Henry IV. Here's what you need to know: a "starveling" is a very thin person. Or scarecrow. An "eel skin" is as you'd imagine: empty, long, wrinkled, thin, and horrible. A "dried neat's tongue" is a dried-up ox tongue. Are you getting it yet? The next one makes it clear. A "bull's pizzle" is a bull's penis. A "stock-fish" is a salted cod. A "tailor's yard" is a yard-long measuring device. A "bow-case" is a long, straight (and again empty) case for a fiddle bow, a "sheath" is a sword holder, and a "vile standing tuck" is a nasty erect sword. Yes, Falstaff is telling Prince Henry he's a bloodless cock.

5. *"Out of my sight! thou dost infect my eyes."†*

---

*Earlier on in the same scene (Act II, scene 4, if you're interested), Henry IV also said: "Did you ever see the sun kiss a dish of butter? The tender-hearted sun, melting the butter with its sweet words! If you have, then take a look at Falstaff." Falstaff, we can assume, was good and sweaty.
†In this play, a character called Margaret, the widow of Henry VI, also lets rip at the Duke of Gloucester with a string of invective that deserves full quotation:

If heaven have any grievous plague in store
Exceeding those that I can wish upon thee,
O, let them keep it till thy sins be ripe,
And then hurl down their indignation

Anne doesn't want to see any more of Richard in *Richard III*. He goes on to reply that her eyes have infected him, and so she hits him with: "Would they were basilisks to strike thee dead." Youch!

4. *"The tartness of his face sours ripe grapes."*

Menenius suggests that Martius doesn't exactly spread positive vibes in *Coriolanus*.

3. *"I do desire we may be better strangers."*

Orlando hits Jacques with a short and sharp one in *As You Like It*.

2. *"Would thou wert clean enough to spit upon."*

Timon here suggests that Apemantus is pretty dirty in *Timon of Athens*. Apemantus goes on to reply that Timon

~~~~~~~~~~~~~~~~

On thee, the troubler of the poor world's peace!
The worm of conscience still begnaw thy soul!
Thy friends suspect for traitors while thou livest,
And take deep traitors for thy dearest friends!
No sleep close up that deadly eye of thine,
Unless it be whilst some tormenting dream
Affrights thee with a hell of ugly devils!
Thou elvish-mark'd, abortive, rooting hog!
Thou that wast seal'd in thy nativity
The slave of nature and the son of hell!
Thou slander of thy mother's heavy womb!
Thou loathed issue of thy father's loins!
Thou rag of honour! thou detested—

Ouchy! Ouchy!

is "too bad to curse." But then Timon gets in the following, even better comeback:

1. *"I'll beat thee, but I would infect my hands."*

After Timon unleashes this beauty, Apemantus tries for "Would thou wouldst burst." After more verbals, Timon declares "I'm sorry I shall lose a stone by thee," and then lobs a rock at him. It's a great scene. Shakespeare! It turns out he could write them …

THE TEN HARSHEST REVIEWS OF OTHERWISE RENOWNED WRITERS

All of these authors have received plenty of praise—but not from everyone.

10. *"It is chloroform in print . . . Whenever [Joseph Smith] found his speech growing too modern—which was about every sentence or two—he ladled in a few such Scriptural phrases as 'exceeding sore,' 'and it came to pass,' etc., and made things satisfactory again. 'And it came to pass' was his pet. If he had left that out, his Bible would have been only a pamphlet."*

Mark Twain reviews Joseph Smith's *The Book of Mormon* in *Roughing It*, 1872.

9. *"The book is crammed with mad, flowery metaphors and hifalutin creative-writing experiments. There are hectic passages on Greek tragedy and the Christian concept of family . . . and heavy Freudian symbolism, including a long description of the removal of a molar, 'a large tooth,' she writes portentously, 'of great personal significance' . . . Acres of poetic whimsy and vague literary blah, a needy, neurotic mandolin solo of reflections on child sacrifice and asides about drains."*

Camilla Long sticks the hatchet into Rachel Cusk's *Aftermath* in 2012.

8. *"Her work is poetry; it must be judged as poetry, and all the weaknesses of poetry are inherent in it."*

The *New York Evening Post* casts the shade on *To the Lighthouse* by Virginia Woolf in 1927.

7. *"Every few years, as a reviewer, one encounters a novel whose ineptitudes are so many in number, and so thoroughgoing, that to explain them fully would produce a text that exceeded the novel itself in both length and interest."*

Robert Macfarlane savages *The Bedroom Secrets of the Master Chefs* by Irvine Welsh in *The New York Times* in 2006.

6. *"And it is that word 'hummy,' my darlings, that marks the first place in* The House at Pooh Corner *at which Tonstant Weader Fwowed up."*

Dorothy Parker takes against *The House at Pooh Corner* by A. A. Milne in *The New Yorker* in 1928.

5. *"Are we in the West so shaken in our sense of ourselves and our culture, are we so disablingly terrified in the face of the various fanaticisms which threaten us, that we can allow ourselves to be persuaded and comforted by such a self-satisfied and, in many ways, ridiculous novel as this?"*

John Banville hands it to Ian McEwan's *Saturday* in the *New York Review of Books* in 2009.

4. *"Every time I read* Pride and Prejudice *I want to dig her up and hit her over the skull with her own shin bone."*

Mark Twain strikes again. This time writing about Jane Austen to his friend W. D. Howells in 1909.

3. *"I remember the players have often mentioned it as an honour to Shakespeare that in his writing, whatever he penned, he never blotted out a line. My answer hath been, 'Would he had blotted a thousand.' "*

Ben Jonson bitches on Shakespeare in 1640.

2. *"I finished* Ulysses *and think it is a mis-fire . . . It is brackish. It is pretentious."*

Virginia Woolf confides her thoughts about James Joyce's magnum opus to her diary in September 1922.

1. *"No man, whose mind has ever been imbued with the smallest knowledge or feeling of classical poetry or classical history, could have stooped to profane and vulgarize every association in the manner which has been adopted by this 'son of promise' . . . Mr Keats is a . . . boy of pretty abilities, which he has done every thing in his power to spoil . . . It is a better and a wiser thing to be a starved apothecary than a starved poet; so back to the shop Mr John, back to 'plasters, pills, and ointment boxes,' &c. But, for Heaven's sake, young Sangrado, be a little more sparing of extenuatives and soporifics in your practice than you have been in your poetry."*

Blackwood's Magazine savages John Keats' *Endymion* in 1818.*

*Poor Keats took a pasting. The *Quarterly Review* said of the same poem: "We have made efforts almost as superhuman as the story itself appears to be, to get through it; but with the fullest stretch of our perseverance, we are forced to confess that we have not been able to struggle beyond the first of the four books ..."

THE TEN MOST REGRETTABLE LITERARY REJECTIONS

It isn't just critics who get it wrong. Publishers too have made some astonishing whoopsies.

10. *"Hopelessly bad"*

A reader report discovered in the archive of Alfred A. Knopf rejecting *Giovanni's Room* by James Baldwin. *The New York Times* review in 1956 said: "His most conspicuous gift is his ability to find words that astonish the reader with their boldness even as they overwhelm him with their rightness." It has remained in print around the world ever since.

9. *"It was not credible. I thought I recognized Nordic figures from mythology, but it seemed a mishmash to me. I couldn't follow it, literally couldn't finish reading it."*

Barney Rosset explains why he rejected J. R. R. Tolkien's *The Lord of the Rings* when he was at Grove Press.

8. *"I'm sorry Mr. Kipling, but you just don't know how to use the English language."*

The *San Francisco Examiner* had bad news for Rudyard Kipling when he filed his second article for them in 1889. Five years later he wrote *The Jungle Book*.

7. *"I like your story, Richard, but nobody in Manhattan can stand it. Time to put it away and go on to your next book."*

Richard Bach's agent had some sad news for his author in 1969. *Jonathan Livingston Seagull* had just been rejected by eighteen publishers. When it was eventually published, it went on to sell 40 million copies.

6. *"Miss Play has a way with words and a sharp eye for unusual and vivid detail. But maybe now that this book is out of her system she will use her talent more effectively next time. I doubt if anyone over here will pick this novel up, so we might well have a second chance."*

Alas, Sylvia Plath (they had even spelled her name wrong) was dead by the time this rejection for her classic novel *The Bell Jar* was written by a reader at Knopf in 1963.

5. *"Very dull . . . a dreary record of typical family bickering, petty annoyances and adolescent emotions . . . Even if the work had come to light five years ago, when the subject was timely, I don't see that there would have been a chance for it."*

Another reader's report. This time encouraging the publisher Alfred A. Knopf to reject the *Diary of Anne Frank* in 1950.

4. *"There is not much demand for animal stories in the USA."*

Dial Press turn down George Orwell's *Animal Farm*, 1944.

3. *"We doubt . . . whether this is the right point of view from which to criticize the political situation at the present time."*

T. S. Eliot at Faber & Faber also rejects *Animal Farm* in the same year.

2. *"I am only one, only one, only one. Only one being, one at the same time. Not two, not three, only one. Only one life to live, only sixty minutes in one hour. Only one pair of eyes. Only one brain. Only one being. Being only one, having only one pair of eyes, having only one time, having only one life, I cannot read your M.S. three or four times. Not even one time. Only one look, only one look is enough. Hardly one copy would sell here. Hardly one. Hardly one."*

Arthur Fifield, founder of the British publishing house A. C. Fifield, thus rejected Gertrude Stein (who famously wrote "a rose is a rose is a rose") in 1912. She is probably still more admired than read today. But she's also been in print for more than a century.

1. *"My dear friend, perhaps I am thick-headed but I just don't understand why a man should take thirty pages to describe how he turns over in his bed before he goes to sleep. It made my head swim."*

Marc Humblot writes to Proust in 1912, turning down *A la recherche du temps perdu* for the Ollendorff publishing house. Thus losing himself the work of a deathless genius.[*]

---

[*]The writer André Gide also turned down Proust's masterpiece for his imprint the *Nouvelle Revue Française*. He later wrote to the author, apologizing. He said that he had committed the "gravest error . . . one of the most burning regrets, remorses, of my life."

THE TEN LONGEST NOVELS

These are books that have been printed by mainstream publishers. Length is here calculated by (approximate[*]) word count. The amount of time they will take out of your life is more variable.[†]

10. *Ponniyin Selvan* by Kalki Krishnamurthy

900,000 words

9. *Kelidar* by Mahmoud Dowlatabadi

950,000 words

8. *Clarissa, or, the History of a Young Lady* by Samuel Richardson

984,870 words

7. *A Dance to the Music of Time* by Anthony Powell

1,000,000 words

---

*Hence the round numbers. There are also often variant editions of these doorstops. Pity the scholars who compare the different texts …
†None of this is to say you shouldn't read these books. Many of them are worth every word. I can personally (and strongly) recommend both Proust and Powell. Plenty of other people enjoy the others. Just be prepared to commit yourself for the long haul.

6. *Zettels Traum* by Arno Schmidt

1,100,000 words

5. *A la recherche du temps perdu* by Marcel Proust

1,267,069 words

4. *Gordana* by Marija Jurić Zagorka

1,400,000 words

3. *Venmurasu** by B. Jeyamohan

1,556,028 words

2. *Het Bureau* by J. J. Voskuil

1,590,000 words

1. *Artamène ou le Grand Cyrus* by Georges and Madeleine de Scudéry

1,954,300 words

*As of August 9, 2016. This Sri Lankan epic is still a work in progress and may soon become the biggest of them all.

CHAPTER 3

UNPOPULAR CULTURE

Music, films, television shows. We surround ourselves with these distracting ephemera because it's better than sitting alone, worrying about death. Or at least, it's meant to be. And yet, there are some aspects of popular culture that really make you question not only the viability of the species, but whether we even deserve to go on.

THE TEN MOST ABUSIVE CLASSICAL MUSIC REVIEWS IN HISTORY*

They might be smarter and quieter than the average rock fan, but no one can twist the knife quite like classical music critics. And they've been sharpening them for centuries …

10. *"We see plainly the savage vulgar faces, we hear curses, we smell vodka. . . . Tchaikovsky's Violin Concerto gives us for the first time the hideous notion that there can be music that stinks to the ear."*

Eduard Hanslick had some reservations about the Vienna premiere of Tchaikovsky's Violin Concerto in December 1881.

9. *"Mahler had not much to say in his Fifth Symphony and occupied a wondrous time in saying it."*

The *New York Sun* did not enjoy Mahler's Fifth in December 1913.

8. *"In search of ear-rending dissonances, torturous transitions, sharp modulations, repugnant contortions of melody and rhythm, Chopin is altogether indefatigable."*

L. Rellstab told readers of *Iris* all about Chopin in Berlin in 1833.

*Several of these quotes (and many, many more gems) can be found in Nicholas Slonimsky's 1953 classic, *Lexicon of Musical Invective*. It's a treasure.

7. *"Beethoven's Second Symphony is a crass monster, a hideously writhing wounded dragon, that refuses to expire, and though bleeding in the Finale, furiously beats about with its tail erect."*

The *Zeitung für die elegante Welt* didn't think much of Ludwig Van's great symphony at its Vienna opening in May 1804.

6. *"Beethoven always sounds to me like the upsettings of bags of nails, with here and there an also dropped hammer."*

Victorian polymath John Ruskin told his friend John Brown he too didn't like Beethoven in a letter from February 1881.

5. *"The faun must have had a terrible afternoon, for the poor beast brayed on muted horns and whinnied on flutes and avoided all trace of soothing melody, until the audience began to share his sorrows."*

Louis Elison lets readers of the *Boston Daily Advertiser* know how much he didn't enjoy Debussy's *Prelude to the Afternoon of a Faun* in 1904.

4. *"Musical impertinence"*

The *Observer* casts shade on Stravinsky's *Rite of Spring* in July 1913.

3. *"We recoil in horror before this rotting odor which rushes into our nostrils from the disharmonies of this putrefactive* *counterpoint. His imagination is so incurably sick and warped that anything like regularity in chord progressions and period structure simply do not exist for him. Bruckner composes like a drunkard!"*

Gustav Dömpke didn't hold back on Anton Bruckner when writing in the *Wiener Allgemeine Zeitung* in March 1886.

2. *"Heartless sterility, obliteration of all melody, all tonal charm, all music . . . This din of brasses, tin pans and kettles, this Chinese or Caribbean clatter with wood sticks and ear-cutting scalping knives . . . This revelling in the destruction of all tonal essence, raging satanic fury in the orchestra, this demoniacal, lewd caterwauling, scandal-mongering, gun-toting music, with an orchestral accompaniment slapping you in the face . . . Hence, the secret fascination that makes it the darling of feeble-minded royalty . . . of the court monkeys covered with reptilian slime, and of the blasé hysterical female court parasites who need this galvanic stimulation by massive instrumental treatment to throw their pleasure-weary frog-legs into violent convulsion."*

J. L. Klein suggested he wasn't Wagner's biggest fan in *The History of Drama*, 1871.

1. *"I played over the music of that scoundrel Brahms. What a giftless bastard! It annoys me that this self-inflated mediocrity is hailed as a genius."*

Tchaikovsky told his diary all about Brahms on October 9, 1886.

THE TEN CRAZIEST PROG ROCK SONG TITLES

I suppose you might grudgingly admire the creativity on display here. And at least these bands weren't spouting the usual nonsense about love and broken hearts. But then again, just look at these:

10. "The Return of the Giant Hogweed"— Genesis (1971)

9. "Cygnus X-1 Book II: Hemispheres"— Rush (1977)

8. "Singring and the Glass Guitar (An Electrified Fairytale)"—Utopia (1977)

7. "Land of the Bag Snake"—Soft Machine (1975)

6. "Duel of the Jester and the Tyrant"—Return to Forever (1976)

5. "The Revealing Science of God (Dance of the Dawn)"—Yes (1973)

4. "Karn Evil 9: 1st Impression, Part 2"— Emerson, Lake & Palmer (1973)

3. "Lady Fantasy"—Camel (1974)

2. "A Plague of Lighthouse Keepers"—Van der Graaf Generator (1971)

1. "Dancing with the Moonlit Knight"—Genesis (1973)

THE WORST DUETS IN POP HISTORY

This list needs no explanation beyond the facts that the 1980s were a terrible time and duets could render even the greatest rock stars awful—let alone soccer stars with atrocious haircuts.[*]

10. "Rabbit"—Chas and Dave (1980)

9. "(Just Like) Starting Over"—John Lennon and Yoko Ono (1980)

8. "Sweet Lovin' Friends"—Sylvester Stallone and Dolly Parton (1984)

7. "Save Your Love"—Renée and Renato (1982)

6. "Especially for You"—Kylie and Jason (1988)

---

*If you really are curious, you can look these tracks up on YouTube. I did when compiling this list, but have a word of advice: don't.

5. "Diamond Lights"—Glenn Hoddle and Chris Waddle (1987)

4. "Say Say Say"—Michael Jackson and Paul McCartney (1983)

3. "The Girl is Mine"—Michael Jackson and Paul McCartney (1982)

2. "Ebony and Ivory"—Stevie Wonder and Paul McCartney (1982)

1. "Dancing in the Street"—Mick Jagger and David Bowie (1985)

THE TEN WORST CHRISTMAS SONGS

This list also needs no explanation.*

10. "Mary's Boy Child"—Cliff Richard (2003)

9. "It's Better to Dream (Christmas Mix)"—Cliff Richard (2016)

8. "Christmas Alphabet"—Cliff Richard (1991)

7. "Have Yourself a Merry Little Christmas"— Cliff Richard (1991)

6. "Santa's List"—Cliff Richard (2003)

5. "Christmas is Quiet"—Cliff Richard (2003)

4. "The Christmas Song"—Cliff Richard (2003)

3. "Saviour's Day"—Cliff Richard (1991)

2. "Mistletoe and Wine"—Cliff Richard (1991)

1. "The Millennium Prayer"—Cliff Richard (1999)

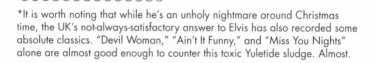

---

*It is worth noting that while he's an unholy nightmare around Christmas time, the UK's not-always-satisfactory answer to Elvis has also recorded some absolute classics. "Devil Woman," "Ain't It Funny," and "Miss You Nights" alone are almost good enough to counter this toxic Yuletide sludge. Almost.

THE WORST ALBUMS OF ALL TIME ACCORDING TO METACRITIC

Metacritic is a website that aggregates scores for reviews and gives them a mark out of 100. To qualify, records have to have received seven or more reviews.[*] This list is naturally skewed toward reviews from after the dawn of the internet. So, the Osmonds and New Kids on the Block are perhaps not fairly represented. Meanwhile, in case you're wondering, the number one album, with a score of 99, is *Ten Freedom Summers* by Wadada Leo Smith.[†]

10. *Fortune*—Chris Brown (2012)

Score: 38

Sample review quote: "Deep listening means getting cozy with a guy so reviled mosquitoes won't bite him."—*Rolling Stone*

9. *Life on Display*—Puddle of Mudd (2012)

Score: 37

Sample review quote: "Third-rate grunge retreads stuffed with overdriven guitars and generic rock-dude melancholia." —*Rolling Stone*

---

*As accessed at http://www.metacritic.com/browse/albums/score/metascore/all/filtered?page=112 on 22 May 2018
†Me neither.

8. *Slick Dogs and Ponies*—Louis XIV (2008)

Score: 37

Sample review quote: "Soulless at its core."—*Slant Magazine*

7. *Nine Track Mind*—Charlie Puth (2016)

Score: 37

Sample review quote: "Whimpers like a sick kitten."—*Q Magazine*

6. *Rebirth*—Lil Wayne (2010)

Score: 37

Sample review quote: "*Rebirth* represents a nightmare fusion of overly processed hip-hop/R&B and dumbed-down rock. Oh well, even Michael Jordan threw up a brick every now and then."—*The Onion* AV Club

5. *One*—Dirty Vegas (2004)

Score: 35

Sample review quote: "Exhaustingly awful"—*Blender*

4. *Testify*—Phil Collins (2002)

Score: 34

Sample review quote: "Middle-age is no excuse for such an unforgivably bland collection of over-emoted love songs."—*Q Magazine*

3. *Famous First Words*—Viva Brother (2011)

Score: 34

Sample review quote: "This album is an abomination."
—*No Ripcord*

2. *Results May Vary*—Limp Bizkit (2003)

Score: 33

Sample review quote: "We've suffered enough."—*NME*

1. *Playing with Fire*—Kevin Federline (2006)

Score: 15

Sample review quote: "The worst thing about *Playing with Fire* is that it's too stale and inept to inspire laughter: it can only elicit weary groans."—Allmusic.com

THE MOST OVERRATED ALBUMS OF ALL TIME

These albums aren't necessarily bad. But nor are they as good as everyone said they were. And there's nothing more disappointing than an overhype.

10. *Is This It*—The Strokes (2001)

No, it isn't it at all.

9. *Timeless*—Goldie (1995)

It's ironic that a record with this title should have dated so badly. Listening to Goldie's pioneering drum 'n' bass now feels like listening to someone doing the washing up in a metal sink—without any water.

8. *Parklife*—Blur (1994)

Blur's most popular and critically acclaimed album is also their worst. More proof that we do not live in a just world.

7. *London Calling*—The Clash (1979)

In three-minute bursts, the Clash are amazing. Over the course of an album, it's like being harangued by a *Socialist Worker* vendor. Only not so funny. Just get "London Calling," the song, "Spanish Bombs," and "Death or Glory," and ignore the rest. Or maybe download "Lover's Rock" too, just to remind you how much of this album is filled with weak reggae filler.

6. *Bitches Brew*—Miles Davis (1969)

Yes, Miles Davis was a genius. Yes, he changed music several times over and yes, this album pushed the frontiers of jazz right off the map. But it's no fun following him there. Critics say: "It's one of the most remarkable creative statements of the last half-century, in any artistic form." I say: "You can't listen to it in the car, can you?" And if you're thinking that's a weak criticism of a mind-blowing record, then just consider what it spawned: the last half century of jazz rock fusion records.

5. *Hotel California*—The Eagles (1976)

Gram Parsons said that listening to the Eagles was like a "dry plastic f*ck." He should have known since it was his country rock template that got them going. But his masterpiece *Grievous Angel* compares to *Hotel California* as drinking champagne does to drinking butt juice. It's yet further proof of the sickness in the world that the Eagles sold so many more records.

4. *BloodSugarSexMagic*—Red Hot Chili Peppers (1991)

Here in the twenty-first century, it's tempting to look on the early 1990s as a golden age. But I have four words to prove that there were problems then too: rap metal funk fusion.

3. *Up the Bracket*—The Libertines (2002)

When people start droning on about "Albion" and authenticity, the correct response is to kick them in the nuts and run, not to treat them like the next Beatles. If critics had been more circumspect, we'd have been spared an awful lot of ugly tabloid escapades.

2. *Definitely Maybe*—Oasis (1994)

If this album is, as we're so often told, the one that defined Britpop, then Britpop was a pint of tepid chemical beer.

1. *The Doors*—The Doors (1967)

Most of this record consists of Jim Morrison giving instructions to women: "light my fire," "let me sleep in your soul kitchen," "go real slow." And when he isn't engaging in casual misogyny he's reeling out nonsense. "All the children are insane," sings the rock and roll poet, "waiting for the summer rain yeah." Yeah? No.

THE WORST ALBUMS BY GREAT ARTISTS

Even Homer nods. And even the greatest rock legends occasionally let slip a loose one …

10. *Having Fun with Elvis on Stage*—Elvis Presley (1974)

This album consists of thirty-seven minutes of Elvis' onstage banter from between songs, accompanied by screams from the crowd. The King's exploitative manager Colonel Tom Parker has a lot to answer for.

9. *Squeeze*—The Velvet Underground (1973)

The fifth album by the Velvet Underground was made without its four founding members, Lou Reed, Sterling Morrison, John Cale, or Maureen Tucker. You can see the problem.

8. *Tales from Topographic Oceans*—Yes (1973)

If you need to know more than that incredible title, I can also tell you that this album has just four twenty-minute songs with lyrics based on ancient Hindu myths. It was too much even for Yes fans.

7. *Cut the Crap*—The Clash (1985)

After Joe Strummer fired the band's lead guitarist, co-lead vocalist, and chief songwriter Mick Jones (alongside drummer Topper Headon), he and the remaining members of The Clash went into the studio determined to show they still had it. The good news is that they avoided the reggae. The bad is that they overloaded their songs with synths and drum machines and recorded this catastrophe. The joke was that "Cut the" should also have been cut from the album's title.

6. *Come*—Prince (1994)

It's saying something that this is the worst record by a man who also recorded a concept album based on the teachings of the Jehovah's Witnesses. Prince really went for it here. He recorded the record as a deliberate attack on his record company Warner Bros and their demands that he give them more music to fulfill his contractual obligations. When the record came out the artist—or The Artist Formerly Known As Prince, as he was now calling himself—derided it in interviews as "old material." It was called "Come," but even he just wanted it to go away.

5. *Everybody's Rockin'*—Neil Young (1983)

Neil Young's twenty-five-minute foray into plastic rockabilly was so bad that his record label tried to sue him. And that's about the only thing anyone remembers about this album today.

4. *Songs from The Capeman*—Paul Simon (1997)

The Capeman was Paul Simon's attempt to make a Broadway musical. It bombed and closed within days, making a loss of more than $10 million. The album actually preceded it down the drain. Simon released it before the musical premiered and it too tanked. Perhaps thanks to lyrics like: "Dom dom dom doo

/ Well-a well I'm home" and a song called "Vampires" in which Dracula's castle is said to look frightening enough to "turn a white man gray" before we get the baffling line: "Made in the shade, use my umbrella."

3. *Dylan and the Dead*—Bob Dylan and the Grateful Dead (1989)

Bob Dylan and the Grateful Dead were two of the greatest acts of their generation. It seemed like an excellent idea to have them work together. What could possibly go wrong? Everything, it turned out.

2. *Metal Machine Music*—Lou Reed (1975)

Guitar feedback. No drums. No singing. No melodies. It was brave. It was innovative. But unfortunately, it was also sh*t.

1. *Never Let Me Down*—David Bowie (1987)

"I didn't really apply myself," Bowie later ruefully reflected on his worst record. "I wasn't quite sure what I was supposed to be doing. I wish there had been someone around who could have told me." Unfortunately, there wasn't. The result was, as he himself called it, his "nadir."

THE WORST BEATLES SONGS

The Beatles never managed an entire album of awful. And generally, there's no point pretending they were any less than great. Which makes this a list of expensive rather than cheap shots. Even so, it's reassuring to think that even the Fab Four could make human errors like the rest of us.

10. "Misery"

Commendable for having a title appropriate to the listening experience it provides—but not much else.

9. "Taxman"

In which multimillionaire, twenty-three-year-old George Harrison complains about giving up any of his money for the public good.

8. "Every Little Thing"

"Every little thing she does, she does for me, yeah." Everything? Are you sure? Does this include picking her nose? Watching *Days of Our Lives*? Licking her fingers to get the last crumbs from a bag of salt and vinegar crisps? Or is she actually an autonomous being?

7. "Within You, Without You"

In which George Harrison now explains that everyone who doesn't share his religious opinions is worse than him.

6. "Komm, Gib Mir Deine Hand"

In 1964, the Fab Four were persuaded to record a German version of one of their biggest hits. When you hear it, you'll understand why they never did it again.

5. "Dig It"

John Lennon said that this was the kind of music you make if you get so stoned you don't give a sh*t. It was so bad that Paul McCartney left it off 2003's remix *Let It Be . . . Naked.*

4. "Free As a Bird"

The musical undead: a mawkish John Lennon session resurrected by the surviving Beatles to promote 1995's *Anthology* albums.

3. "Ob-La-Di, Ob-La-Da"

Stupid title, stupid song.

2. "I Saw Her Standing There"

"Well she was just seventeen, well you know what I mean …" No, Sir Paul, I'm not sure I do. Could you elaborate?

1. "Maxwell's Silver Hammer"

Not only the worst song by the Beatles, but maybe the most irritating song of all time. The evil of this absurd earworm must be multiplied by the number of times it will loop around your protesting head following every occasion when you are unlucky enough to hear it.

THE TEN LEAST STREAMED BEATLES SONGS ON SPOTIFY

As compiled by Vulture.com in December 2015, based on Spotify's public streaming counts from the Beatles' otherwise all-conquering popular first week on the streaming service.

10. "Honey Don't"

9. "Thank You Girl"

8. "I'll Get You"

7. "Long Tall Sally"

6. "I Call Your Name"

5. "The Inner Light"

4. "Slow Down"

3. "Bad Boy"

2. "Matchbox"

1. "Her Majesty"*

---

*Neatly, "Her Majesty" was the last song on their last album, *Abbey Road*. A bizarre twenty-six-second smidge of sound coming in after (the far more magisterial) "The End." Most of the other songs here are early B-sides. Which is why you might not have heard of them either.

THE WORST SONGS BY FORMER BEATLES

Contrary to what you may have been told, the post-breakup legacy of former Beatles is often pretty excellent. Paul McCartney's *Ram*,[*] John Lennon's Plastic Ono Band, George Harrison's "All Things Must Pass." These are classics. And there are many more. Even Ringo had his moments. But the following tracks go a long way to explaining why so many people think so little of those solo careers.

10. "Woman is the Nigger of the World" — John Lennon (1972)

A song so stupid that even describing it brings a contamination risk. The title tells you most of what you need to know. There's also a sax solo.

9. "Teardrops" — George Harrison (1981)

If you listen to this synth-drenched nonsense,[†] you'll find it almost impossible to imagine it came from the same pen that composed "Something." "It feels like I've taken over from the rain," drones Harrison over game-show organ trills. Shut up, quiet Beatle.

---

[*] And make sure you look up Paul McCartney's Fireman recordings. They're wild.
[†] But don't!

8. "Imagine"—John Lennon (1971)

So saccharine it could rot an elephant's teeth. Also: "imagine no possessions"? It's easy if you're rich. I'll have that fancy white grand piano you're using to bang out this crap for a start.

7. "Bip Bop"*—Paul McCartney (1971)

John Lennon is most often accused of putting out any old nonsense and assuming people would be interested. But "Bip Bop" sounds like an outtake of an outtake of a jam session gone wrong. "The song just goes nowhere. I still cringe every time I hear it." So said Sir Paul McCartney and who would want to argue with him?

6. "Cambridge 1969"—John Lennon (1969)

Twenty-six minutes of dissonant feedback, arhythmic cymbal bashing, and Yoko Ono screeching and screaming. It's impressively out there—but I defy you to listen to all of it. "Utter bullsh*t" said *Rolling Stone* magazine.

5. "Drumming is My Madness"—Ringo Starr (1981)

Ringo may have been a far better drummer than people often give him credit for, but even before he started supporting Brexit there was evidence that Ringo was not the brightest Beatle. The fact that he decided to record this song was a case in point.

---

*This track comes from the much-maligned first Wings album. Which is actually surprisingly excellent.

"Drumming makes me lose control," sings Ringo, while sounding ironically bored and flat. To make matters worse, it's rumored that he didn't actually bother to play drums on the track.

4. "Motor of Love"—Paul McCartney (1989)

A love song slopped out with enough treacle to bog down a tank battalion. This is the nadir of McCartney's sentimental eighties gloop. Which is saying something.

3. "Unconsciousness Rules"—George Harrison (1981)

Fancy hearing a lecture from George Harrison about the perils of going to the "discotheque" set against a soft rock honky-tonk piano backdrop? Me neither. There's also a sax solo. Of course there is.

2. "The No, No Song"—Ringo Starr (1974)

This song about not taking drugs writes its own review. Which is the only good thing you can say about it.

1. *Wedding Album*, side one—John Lennon (1969)

Twenty-two minutes of John calling out Yoko's name, and Yoko calling John, both of them in various states of agitation. During all that time you'd think that one of them might have answered and we'd have been spared this nonsense.

THE WORST TV SHOWS OF ALL TIME

It's television that makes me feel saddest for any alien civilizations that may be monitoring us. A solid 99 percent of everything we beam out is appalling dreck, which makes this list of outstandingly bad transmissions all the more egregious.

10. *The Cosby Show* (1984–1992)

At the time it was aired, plenty of people liked this warm depiction of middle-class African Americans. But the idea of serial rapist Bill Cosby delivering moral lessons makes it impossible to watch now. And far less cozy …

9. *Game of Thrones* (2011—present)

Okay: this is minority view. But. Swords with names: check. Exploitative nudity to divert you from the fact that everything else that's happening is boring: check. People able to give birth to demons who can kill anyone, who then only use said demons to kill one individual when they could have kicked serious ass and neatly wrapped everything up in season three: check. *Game of Thrones* is just an expensive brand of silly. With nudity.

8. *The Apprentice* (2004–2017)

Donald Trump said that reality TV was for "the bottom feeders of society," which he went on to prove by hosting this program about testing business skills for fourteen seasons. It was here that the concept of Trumponomics was born and he began to build the profile that would enable him to become president. So, when he finally loses his sh*t and hits the nuclear button, we'll have crap TV to blame.

7. *The Alex Jones Show* (2011–present)

Your go-to resource for nonsense about chemtrails, government weather control programs, lies about mass shootings being "false flag" operations, lots and lots of shouting, and adverts for bogus vitamin supplements. Only less entertaining than all that sounds.

6. *The Wright Way* (2013)

Yes, *The Wright Way* was an ironic title for a program that went so very wrong. Ben Elton, who helped create classics like *The Young Ones* and *Blackadder*, decided to take on "health and safety culture." The result was like a live action *Daily Mail* article—and just as nightmarish. The *Daily Mirror* called it "the worst sitcom ever."

5. *The O'Reilly Factor* (1996–2017)

For eleven years Bill O'Reilly lied about American politics, was rude to guests, told victims of terrorist attacks to "shut up," spread right-wing conspiracy theories, claimed gay marriage would lead to "interspecies" unions, and harassed women behind the scenes. He wasn't very nice.

4. *Triangle* (1981)

A soap opera set on board a North Sea ferry and recorded on primitive video tape recorders. What could go wrong? Yes, everything. The awful weather made it perpetually gray. The sound was muffled and actors had to contend against the hum of the boat's engine. The cameras didn't work properly either: there were problems with light, color variations and wobble, and even the speed of the film was inconsistent. Watching episodes on YouTube is an endurance challenge to rival eating all the tarmac on the M6.

3. *Naked Jungle* (2000)

Poor old Keith Chegwin (Cheggers), once a children's TV star, now wearing nothing except a hat and chasing naturists over an assault course. "It's the worst career move I made in my entire life," said Cheggers. The prestigious listings guide the *Radio Times* said: "It's the worst British TV programme ever." But that was in 2006. And after that there came …

2. *Mrs Brown's Boys* (2011–present)

Everything you need to know about the UK's decision to leave the EU is explained by the popularity of this program. It has all gone wrong.

1. *Jim'll Fix It* (1975–1994)

Like *The Cosby Show*, this program about making kids' dreams come true was surprisingly popular when it aired. But pedophile Jimmy Savile turned out not to be the ideal frontman.

THE TEN BIGGEST FAILURES ON BROADWAY

Getting a show up and running on Broadway is among the highest achievements in theatre. As the song says, if you can make it there, you can make it anywhere. But of course, not everyone does.

10. *Carrie* (1988)

Performances: 5

This adaption of Stephen King's hit book (which had also been a successful film) cost $8 million to stage. But there were foreseeable problems recreating Carrie's telekinetic powers. There was a lot of stuff floating around on strings—and that just made audiences laugh. "Puppetry has its uses," wrote David Richards in the *Washington Post*, "although advancing terror is not one of them." Oh, and the producers decided to turn the horror story into a musical: "A low water-mark of the genre" according to *The New Yorker*.

9. *Prymate* (2004)

Performances: 5

A play about scientists fighting over a gorilla. "Connoisseurs of see-it-or-regret-it theatrical disasters will want to make tracks to the Longacre Theater, and fast, to catch *Prymate*," advised *Variety*. But not enough of them got there fast enough.

8. *Bring Back Birdie* (1981)

Performances: 4

The sequel to *Bye Bye Birdie*, a successful show from 1961. But twenty years after the original, no one was interested and *The New York Times* said it was "depressing and tired."

7. *The Apple Doesn't Fall* (1996)

Performances: 1

In a plot "soggy with contrivance" according to *Variety*, a sitcom writer enrolls her mother in an experimental drug program after discovering she has Alzheimer's. Yuckily, she then falls for her mother's doctor. *The New York Times* said it was "ghastly."

6. *Kelly* (1965)

Performances: 1

A reimagining of the story of Steve Brodie, who jumped off the Brooklyn Bridge in 1886 and survived. Walter Kerr described the performance he saw as "a bad idea gone wrong." And even before the show opened the writers had sued the producers. One of the lead actors was also written out at the last minute. *The New York Times* congratulated her for thus avoiding a farce in its scathing review.

5. *Oldest Living Confederate Widow Tells All* (2003)

Performances: 1

A one-woman show based on Alan Gurganus' 700-page novel about a ninety-nine-year-old woman recalling her marriage to a Civil War veteran. Its previews had scathing notices and when the show opened and closed in one night, *Playbill* ran with the headline: "The Oldest Confederate Widow Tells No More."

4=. *First One Asleep Whistle* (1966)

Performances: 1

4=. *Father's Day* (1971)

Performances: 1

4=. *I Won't Dance* (1981)

Performances: 1

First One Asleep Whistle, *I Won't Dance*, and *Father's Day* were all written by Oliver Hailey, labeled in *The New York Times* as "the most produced, least successful playwright" on Broadway. He appears to have been sanguine about his failures. According to his wife, he said that at least "they ran all evening."

1. *Moose Murders* (1983)

Performances: 1

A mystery farce involving incest and a man who kicks a moose in its private area. The people who attended were astonished. "Those of us who have witnessed the play that opened at the Eugene O'Neill Theater last night will undoubtedly hold periodic reunions, in the noble tradition of survivors of the *Titanic*," said *The New York Times*. Twenty-five years after the show's infamous opening and swift closing, the paper also called it: "the standard of awfulness against which all Broadway flops are judged."

THE TEN WORST FILMS OF ALL TIME ACCORDING TO METACRITIC*

Metacritic, the website that aggregates scores for reviews, covers films as well as albums. To qualify, the films have to have received seven or more reviews. Again, this list skews toward works that were made after the arrival of the internet. So no Ed Wood. But that doesn't mean *The Human Centipede* is any less awful. Scores are out of 100. (At the other end of the scale, *Citizen Kane*, *The Godfather*, *Rear Window*, *Casablanca*, *Boyhood*, and *Three Colours: Red* all received 100.)

10. *Baby Geniuses* (1999)

Director: Bob Clark

Score: 6

Plot summary: Two doctors crack the code to baby language. The babies turn out to be geniuses and try to take over the world. But mainly they just seem to talk about "diaper gravy."

Sample review quote: "A horrible, horrible film that wears out its welcome before its opening credits." Nathan Rabin, *The Onion AV Club*

9. *National Lampoon's Gold Diggers* (2004)

Director: Gary Preisler

Score: 6

---

*As accessed on May 17, 2018 at http://www.metacritic.com/browse/movies/score/metascore/all/filtered?page=111

Plot summary: Two dreadful men marry old ladies so they can take their fortunes when they die.

Sample review quote: "So prodigiously unintriguing that audiences could be forgiven for stampeding from theaters to strangle its writer-director, Gary Preisler, in his sleep." Tim Appelo, *LA Weekly*

8. *The Human Centipede III* (Final Sequence) (2015)

Director: Tom Six

Score: 5

Plot summary: A prison warden tries to impress a hard-ass local governor by stitching inmates together mouth to anus.

Sample review quote: "If you hate movies, and you find sexual assault funny, *The Human Centipede III: Final Sequence* should meet your needs." Robert Abele, *LA Times*

7. *Vulgar* (2002)

Director: Bryan Johnson

Score: 5

Plot summary: A clown doesn't have much luck entertaining children so starts telling rude jokes at stag parties.

Sample review quote: "Sure to appear in everyone's worst-of lists at year's end, to say nothing of a few bad dreams, Bryan Johnson's *Vulgar* is an unclassifiably awful study in self- and audience-abuse." Mark Holcomb, *Village Voice*

6. *Strippers* (2000)

Director: Jorge Ameer

Score: 2

Plot summary: An advertising executive is stripped of everything he owns, including his life.

Sample review quote: "Unbelievably awful celluloid waster." V. A. Musetto, *New York Post*

5. *Hillary's America: The Secret History of The Democratic Party* (2016)

Director: Bruce Schooley and Dinesh D'Souza

Score: 2

Plot summary: Hillary Clinton is bad because it was the Republicans who abolished slavery during the Civil War over 150 years ago.

Sample review quote: "The cinematic equivalent of a drunk man at a sports bar sucking back whole jalapeño peppers hoping for applause without ever being dared." Jordan Hoffman, *The Guardian*

4. *The Singing Forest* (2003)

Director: Jorge Ameer[*]

Score: 1

Plot summary: Two gay lovers who were murdered during the Holocaust are reincarnated and one of them becomes the lover

---

[*]Yes, the person who made *Strippers* got to direct another film.

of the other's daughter. (Seriously. That's the story. I only wish I was making this stuff up.)

Sample review quote: "Provides scant entertainment value, intentional or otherwise . . . [Its] problems leave no department untouched." Dennis Harvey, *Variety*

3. *United Passions* (2015)

Director: Frédéric Auburtin

Score: 1

Plot summary: A feature bankrolled by sports organization FIFA extoling the brilliance of, erm, FIFA and its disgraced president Sebb Blatter.

Sample review quote: "As cinema it is excrement. As proof of corporate insanity it is a valuable case study." Jordan Hoffman, *The Guardian*

2. *Bio-Dome* (1996)

Director: Jason Bloom

Score: 1

Plot summary: Two stoners on a road trip go for a bathroom stop in what they think is a shopping mall, but turns out to be a bio-dome full of scientists which is about to be sealed off for a year. Which about as long as the ensuing comedy of errors seems to last if you're unlucky enough to watch it.

Sample review quote: "Malodorous . . . A non-stop moronathon." Hal Hinson, *Washington Post*

1. *Chaos* (2005)

Director: David DeFalco

Score: 1

Plot summary: Two teenage girls on the way to a rave in some woods are tortured and killed.

Sample review quote: "The only thing this so-called cautionary tale will inspire audiences to do is to never sit through another insultingly awful piece of exploitative trash "conceived" by David DeFalco." Laura Kern, *The New York Times*

THE TEN BIGGEST BOX OFFICE BOMBS

Hollywood is often criticized for not taking enough risks. But losses like these make you understand why the money men might be nervous.

10. *Supernova* (2000)

Loss adjusted for inflation: $118 million (Loss at time: $83 million)

9. *Stealth* (2005)

Loss adjusted for inflation: $120 million (Loss at time: $96 million)

8. *Heaven's Gate* (1980)

Loss adjusted for inflation: $120 million (Loss at time: $40.5 million)

7. *The Alamo* (2004)

Loss adjusted for inflation: $122 million (Loss at time: $94 million)

6. *John Carter* (2012)

Loss adjusted for inflation: $130 million (Loss at time: $122 million)

5. *Final Fantasy: The Spirits Within* (2001)

Loss adjusted for inflation: $130 million (Loss at time: $94 million)

4. *The Adventures of Pluto Nash* (2002)

Loss adjusted for inflation: $131 million (Loss at time: $96 million)

3. *Titan A.E.* (2000)

Loss adjusted for inflation: $142 million (Loss at time: $100 million)

2. *Cutthroat Island* (1995)

Loss adjusted for inflation: $143 million (Loss at time: $89 million)

1. *Sinbad: Legend of the Seven Seas* (2003)

Loss adjusted for inflation: $166 million (Loss at time: $125 million)

THE WORST WACKY SIDEKICKS IN POPULAR MOVIE FRANCHISES

How wuude!

10. Jar-Jar Binks

9. Jar-Jar Binks

8. Jar-Jar Binks

7. Jar-Jar Binks

6. Jar-Jar Binks

5. Jar-Jar Binks

4. Jar-Jar Binks

3. Jar-Jar Binks

2. Jar-Jar Binks

1. Jar-Jar Binks

THE TEN WORST WINNERS OF THE BEST PICTURE OSCAR

The Oscars are supposed to be the ultimate accolade. Which makes the awards given to these films all the more perplexing.

10. *Out of Africa* (1985)

In the mid-1980s, the Academy loved dishing out gongs to worthy but uncomfortably patronizing stories about life under the British Empire. This is one of the longest and slowest of the genre. Even Meryl Streep and Robert Redford can't make it interesting.

9. *Around the World in 80 Days* (1956)

This big budget extravaganza contains over forty celebrity cameos. That's right. Forty of them. And it turns out that celebrity cameos were just as bad in the 1950s. Worse, in fact, if you consider that you won't have a clue why most of the people mugging at the camera in this interminable old farce were ever famous.

8. *The Great Ziegfeld* (1936)

If you haven't heard of this film, you aren't alone. Few people watch it now—and for good reason. It's regarded as overblown, overlong, and underwhelming. It's a historical curiosity as a picture that used to be one of the most highly regarded films of all time back in the 1930s. But the only question it really answers is whether films used to be worse than they are now. The answer is yes.

7. *Cavalcade* (1933)

This drama about posh English people and their plucky servants helped start a poisonous screen tradition in the UK of glamourizing class inequalities and a mythical past. The same tradition that brought us *Downton Abbey* and Brexit.

6. *Ben-Hur* (1959)

Chop out the chariot race and it's abysmal. Two hundred minutes worth of sanctimonious religious drama.

5. *Dances with Wolves* (1990)

If you like Kevin Costner over-emoting, you're in luck. There's a healthy three hours worth of mullet shredding here. But you're going to be less pleased if you don't like patronizing depictions of Native Americans. And films that are almost as stupid as their title.

4. *The Broadway Melody* (1929)

The Broadway Melody was pretty much the first musical comedy and although it's now considered awful, it was a critical and commercial smash. It therefore established the long, painful tradition of Hollywood musicals getting undue praise and attention. Getting made at all, in fact. Just think, if it wasn't for his film we might have escaped *The Greatest Showman* and *Annie*.

3. *Shakespeare in Love* (1998)

It may be about Shakespeare, but that doesn't mean it's clever. Part of the plot hinges around the Bard struggling to come up with the plot for *Romeo and Juliet*, when everyone who's studied it in English class knows that in reality he just adapted an existing story. The rest is a stupid love story so soppy you could use it to clean an entire football team.

2. *Titanic* (1997)

The boat sank. There you go. I've just spared you having to sit through three hours of histrionics, schlock, and patronizing renditions of Irish jigs.

1. *Braveheart* (1995)

Okay, films don't have a duty to be accurate, but you'd think the Academy might at least have noticed that Mel Gibson's rendering of the Battle of Stirling Bridge doesn't even have a bridge in it. Worse still, *Braveheart* is quite possibly the most racist film to win an Oscar. Which is saying something. Its raging xenophobia may be directed at everyone's favorite villains, the English, but that doesn't make it any more pleasant.

THE WORST LINES IN FILMS

There's nothing like a good one-liner to lift a film script. And these are nothing like good one-liners.

10. *"A bird may love a fish, signore, but where will they live?"*

A question that provokes yet more questions from Danielle in *Ever After: A Cinderella Story* (1998).

9. *"It's a pressure valve. It won't open unless there's tremendous pressure."*

Robert Ramsey explains the basics in *Poseidon* (2006).

8. *"They're aiding the return of the Dark Lord so he can slaughter billions and enslave the survivors to serve him in a new age of Magic. They're Inferni. They destroyed the Illuminati a hundred years ago. I too am Inferni, but I escaped. The Shield of Light hid me. Liela gave an assassin her wand to kill me. But I got the wand from her. Keep it away from Liela. She mustn't get her wand back. With it she can restore the Dark Lord's power."*

Tikka explains (and explains) the not-so-basics in *Bright* (2017).

7. *"Inspector Clay is dead, murdered, and somebody's responsible."*

Lieutenant John Harper isn't exactly wrong in *Plan 9 from Outer Space* (1959).*

---

*Ed Wood's infamous masterpiece also gave us this astonishing bit of scene

6. *"We finally got to the boat . . . But it wasn't there."*

Rudy is probably wrong in *House of the Dead* (2003).

5. *"Pain don't hurt."*

Dalton is definitely wrong in *Road House* (1989).

4. *"At least he won't be using heroin-flavoured bananas to finance revolution."*

James Bond has something to celebrate in *Goldfinger* (1964).

3. *"I don't like sand. It's coarse and rough and irritating and it gets everywhere."*

Doesn't Anakin Skywalker have bigger things to worry about in *Star Wars: Episode II—Attack of the Clones* (2002)?

2. *"Your eyes are amazing, do you know that? You should never shut them, not even at night."*

Paul Martel's pick-up line is not only nauseating, it's singularly bad advice for his love interest in *Unfaithful* (2002).

1. *"I like nice tits. I always have, how about you?"*

Cristal Connors demonstrates the intellectual level of *Showgirls* (1995).

---

setting: "Greetings, my friend. We are all interested in the future, for that is where you and I are going to spend the rest of our lives. And remember my friend, future events such as these will affect you in the future."

THE WORST SEX SCENES IN MOVIES

Ten scenes that set audiences around the world squirming—but not in a good way.

10. *Basic Instinct 2* (2006)

Rather impractically, Stan Collymore and Sharon Stone get their freak on while driving through Canary Wharf at top speed in a sports car. The streets are conveniently empty, but it's still difficult not to worry more about pedestrians than it is about Stan finding release.

9. *Body of Evidence* (1993)

Arguably, the top of a stationary car is safer than a moving one. But this interaction between Willem Defoe and Madonna is rendered laughably dumb when Madge smashes a lightbulb[*] on said roof then encourages Defoe to roll around on it. This moment helped her to win the worst actress awards at the Razzies.

8. *Showgirls* (1995)

This scene also helped win a Razzie, this time for the unfortunate Elizabeth Berkley who partners up with Kyle MacLachlan in a swimming pool. It wasn't just the horror of seeing the actor who played Agent Cooper doing the nasty that upset audiences, it was

---

*I don't know why she brought a lightbulb to a seduction either.

the way Berkley started flipping around on MacLachlan's rod like a fish in its death throes. It's one of those awful moments that has to be seen to be believed, but also isn't worth the mental pain of witnessing.

7. *The Counselor* (2013)

To finally ram home the point about how wrong scenes involving sex and cars can go, Cameron Diaz plays a character who rubs her ladyparts against the windscreen of a Ferrari while Javier Bardem gawks at her from the inside. This won her the not-so-coveted "Actress Most in Need of a New Agent" award from the Alliance of Women Film Journalists.

6. *The Room* (2003)

According to the book *The Disaster Artist*, actor-director Tommy Wiseau declared: "I have to show my ass or this movie won't sell." Which explains why there are so many long and disturbing shots of his pumping buttocks. What it doesn't explain is why in several shots he appears to be trying to have sex with a young woman's navel. I've been told that's not how it's done.

5. *Munich* (2005)

While having sex, and bellowing like a lost cow, Eric Bana's character has flashbacks to the Munich massacre. These grow more violent as Bana approaches his screaming loud climax, but the result is far more hilarious than dramatic. This is almost certainly Steven Spielberg's worst bit of direction.

4. *Taking Lives* (2004)

Angelina Jolie and Ethan Hawke make the beast with two backs on top of a chest of drawers. As if that weren't challenging enough, Ethan Hawke's character performs his acrobatics fully clothed. Angelina Jolie, meanwhile, had to get fully naked in an unintentional parody of the inequitable dynamics of Hollywood.

3. *Gigli* (2003)

"It's turkey time," says Jennifer Lopez.
"Huh?" says Ben Affleck, speaking for many.
"Gobble, gobble," replies JLo. As if that isn't bad enough, she adds: "Lay some of that sweet hetero-lingus on me."

2. *Howard the Duck* (1986)

Talking of fowl language, no one wants to hear an animated duck discuss his "appreciation" of the "female version of the human anatomy," let alone watch him get into bed with Lea Thompson and start to "go for it."

1. *Avatar* (2009)

Two twelve-feet-tall, blue, cartoon humanoids . . . Actually, that's probably all the information you need.

THE TEN MOST PREPOSTEROUS ROMANTIC COMEDY PLOTLINES

There's a school of thought that says romantic comedies take a lot of skill to make and never quite get the critical acclaim they deserve. There's also a school of thought that looks at these plotlines and wonders: what the hell is wrong with everyone?

10. *Kissin' Cousins* (1964)

Elvis Presley appears both as an air force officer and his hillbilly cousin. Alas, the title is otherwise misleading and we don't get to see the King kissin' himself. Instead, Air Force Elvis falls for a beautiful hillbilly, the hillbilly Elvis falls for a woman in the air force, everything gets mixed up, and much hilarity doesn't ensue.

9. *The Beautician and the Beast* (1997)

A New York beautician's studio burns down after a student she is teaching ignites some hairspray with a cigarette. So, when she is hired (by mistake—it's a long story) as a teacher for an Eastern European dictator's children in a country called, wait for it, Slovetzia, she goes. And that's when it starts to get really silly. She falls in love with the dictator, he falls out of love with terrorizing his home population, they get together, and a new democratic dawn breaks over Slovetzia. All of this crap is what happens when you think of a funny title and then force the plot to fit around it.[*]

***

[*] "Funny" used in its broadest sense.

8. *Grease 2* (1982)

Sandy's English cousin . . . That's right. Her cousin. From England. The one who definitely wasn't mentioned in the first film. And only appears because most of the original cast were absent from this nonsense. Anyway, Sandy's English cousin comes to Rydell High. He's a bit nerdy for the head of the Pink Ladies, so becomes a "cool" motorcycle rider. But he does so in disguise and keeps failing to tell his love interest about his outlaw life and people sing songs about reproduction in biology lessons and some bad guys called the Cycle Lords keep getting into fights with Sandy's cousin and there are more songs about Hula. And then, mercifully, it ends.

7. *Rumor Has It* (2005)

Jennifer Aniston plays a woman who is told that her mother and grandmother inspired the film *The Graduate*. And that her mother slept with a guy called Beau (played by Kevin Costner) just before her wedding, a bit like in the Dustin Hoffman classic. So Jennifer Aniston decides Kevin Costner is therefore most likely her father. So she tracks him down. And sleeps with him. And the worst thing is that it's only after this apparent incest that the film really goes off the rails ...

6. *The Switch* (2010)

Jennifer Aniston (again!) plays a woman whose best friend Wally empties out a cup of sperm intended for her insemination and fills it with his own love juice. She gives birth to Wally's child rather than the child of the man she'd intended to have a baby with. Wally eventually admits to the misdeed he's, ahem, pulled off. And soon afterward Aniston marries him anyway.

5. *Just Go with It* (2011)

Poor old Jennifer Aniston is now made to pretend to be a woman eager to bed Adam Sandler. Brooklyn Decker wants to bed him too. That's right: Adam Sandler. "Just go with it" is presumably what their agents said.

4. *Mannequin Two: On the Move* (1991)

Kirsty Swanson plays a peasant girl who was turned into a mannequin 1,000 years ago by a wizard with a magic necklace. In the present day, she is placed in the window of a store. A guy called Jason, played by William Ragsdale, removes the necklace. It soon emerges that he's descended from a prince—but look out! The descendant of the sorcerer is also around and wants to take the peasant girl and magic necklace to Bermuda. Honestly. That's what happens.

3. *Say It Isn't So* (2001)

Heather Graham and Chris Klein play young lovers who come to believe they are siblings. This yucky scenario is then played for laughs. Which don't come. Chris Klein also puts his hand up a cow's butt. Which is a pretty good image to describe the state of this film.

2. *Blame It on Rio* (1984)

At least *Say It Isn't So* didn't try to squeeze laughs out of borderline pedophilia. The same can't be said for *Blame It on Rio*, in which two middle-aged dads sleep with each other's teenage daughters. One of those daughters is then shown trying to commit suicide by eating too many birth control pills. And that isn't even the dumbest scene.

1. *The Hottie and the Nottie* (2008)

Paris Hilton is very attractive. But she's still single because she hangs out with a not-hot friend. Men recoil at the sight of this poor woman. Until she scrubs up and turns out to be hot too. And, therefore, also gets a shot at happiness. The critic Mark Kermode called it a "disgusting . . . fascist eugenic tract."* Which is putting it mildly.

---

*It's safe to say that critics did not enjoy this film. The *Village Voice* described it as: "crass, shrill, disingenuous, tawdry, mean-spirited, vulgar, idiotic, boring, slapdash, half-assed, and very, very unfunny." In the *Miami Herald*, Connie Ogle said: "Imagine the worst movie you've ever seen. Got it? Now try to think of something worse. That something is this movie—wretched, embarrassing and a waste of the time and energy of everyone involved."

CHAPTER 4

THE STATE OF OUR NATIONS

This genuinely rough guide to the world and its leading cities gives you the facts and figures you need to help you make up your mind about places you don't want to visit and where you probably wouldn't like to live.

THE MOST EXPENSIVE PINT OF BEER IN THE WORLD BY CITY

Ranked according to Deutsche Bank's 2017 Mapping the World's Prices survey, in US dollars according to exchange rates at the time. Looking on the bright side, this list does finally give us a reason to feel sorry for Norwegians, instead of just envying them.

10. Auckland, New Zealand—$6.5

9. Melbourne, Australia—$6.7

8. Zurich, Switzerland—$6.7

7. Stockholm, Sweden—$6.9

6. Paris, France—$7.2

5. Boston, USA—$7.2

4. New York City, USA—$7.4

3. Hong Kong, China—$7.7

2. Singapore—$9.0

1. Oslo, Norway—$9.9

THE WORST PLACES TO GO ON VACATION

Here are the ten least competitive tourist destinations, according to the World Economic Forum Travel & Tourism Competitiveness Index 2017.* The WEF allots countries a mark based upon factors like safety and security, health and hygiene, environmental sustainability, transport infrastructure, and cultural resources. For reference, in 2017, Spain came top with a mark of 5.43—it's sunny and the food is great. At the other end of the scale, Yemen was on fire, subject to brutal bombing campaigns, civil war, and troop incursions from Saudi Arabia.

10. Benin—2.84

9. Lesotho—2.84

8. Nigeria—2.82

7. Mali—2.78

6. Sierra Leone—2.69

5. Mauritania—2.64

4. Democratic Republic of Congo—2.64

3. Burundi—2.57

2. Chad—2.52

1. Yemen—2.44

*"Least competitive" is bureaucrat-speak for "worst."

THE TEN MOST EXPENSIVE DESTINATIONS IN THE WORLD

The World Economic Forum Travel & Tourism Competitiveness Index 2017 gives destinations a score out of ten based on ticket taxes and airport charges, hotel price index, purchasing power parity, and fuel prices. The good news for Londoners is that Brexit will soon have the UK capital crashing out of this list. The bad news is that they won't be able to escape to Europe any more.

10. Peru—3.83

9. Australia—3.82

8. Denmark—3.75

7. Senegal—3.75

6. Norway—3.69

5. Iceland—3.58

4. Israel—3.13

3. Barbados—3.05

2. United Kingdom—2.83

1. Switzerland—2.81

THE TEN WORST US CITIES FOR BEDBUGS

This list was compiled by pest control services company Orkin, LLC in January 2018. In case you're wondering, the best way to get rid of bedbugs is to BURN EVERYTHING. Burn your sheets, your furniture, your clothes, your house. Then gather the ashes, send them into space, nuke them, bring them back down, and burn them again.

10. Dallas

9. San Francisco

8. New York

7. Detroit

6. Cincinnati

5. Columbus (Ohio)

4. Los Angeles

3. Chicago

2. Washington DC

1. Baltimore

THE WORLD'S MOST PITIABLE COMMUTES

I could have listed your own personal commute as the number one contender. After all, it is likely to bring with it many of the disadvantages listed here, topped off by the fact that once you have completed it, you will also have to spend a day at work. But while I sympathize with your struggles, I also ask you to spare a thought for the people battling through these overcrowded cities.

10. Moscow

Rush hour travel takes 44 percent longer than normal travel in Moscow, making it one of the world's most congested cities. Plus your chances of being stuck in traffic while passing through a depressing and dangerous concrete nightmare are uncomfortably high.

9. San Francisco

In 2014, commuting in San Francisco became so fraught that protesters began stoning the private luxury buses that were ferrying workers between the city and the offices of tech companies like Google in Silicon Valley.* Meanwhile, the city's surroundings have become notorious for the ninety-minute-plus

---

*In classic tech-company style, these buses used the same stops and infrastructure as public transport buses (thus adding to delays and congestion) but were not open to the public. Nor did they pay fees to city government. Meanwhile, house prices started going up around the bus stops. More people from Silicon Valley moved to San Francisco . . . And more rocks were thrown.

"super-commutes" that 10 percent of residents have to endure every day. And commute times have been rising at an unhealthy 17 percent in the decade leading up to 2018.

8. Jakarta

A typical commuter in Indonesia's capital faces 400 hours a year in traffic. There are 1.38 million of these average commuters. Meaning over 80,000 lifetimes are eaten up on the city's roads every year.[*]

7. Mumbai

The average summer temperature in Mumbai is around 90 degrees Fahrenheit. It often tops off at over 104 degrees. During the monsoon months of July and August, relative humidity stands at 86 percent. Average rainfall comes in at around 33 in.[†] Meanwhile, 12 million people have to complete a daily commute through these conditions.

6. Rio de Janeiro

According to a 2018 survey by Expert Market, commuters in Rio spend an average of an hour and a half getting to work. Drivers spend 51 hours a year in traffic.

---

[*]I did the math so you don't have to: 400 x 1.38 million = 552 million. The average life contains 672,000 hours. (Don't think about that for too long. You don't want to waste that precious time after all ...)
[†]On July 26, 2005, over 37 in. fell in one brutal day.

5. Istanbul

In 2015, TomTom ran a traffic survey declaring Istanbul the most congested city in the world. It stated that a rush hour drive takes at least twice as long as at quieter times. And that residents enjoy 125 hours a year waiting in traffic jams.

4. Ho Chi Minh City

There are 37 million motorcycles in Vietnam. Most of them are in the capital. Most of those are at screaming full pelt at rush hour. So don't even think about crossing the road.

3. Mexico City

Tezcatlipoca was the local Aztec god in the Mexico City area. His name meant "smoking mirror" and he governed chance and destiny. He was also known as Necoc Yaotl, "the Enemy of Both Sides." Under his rule, nothing was certain. And

his influence remains strong. For instance, the numbers of buildings in many streets do not even follow sequential order. (It's quite possible to see a house number 64 with numbers 50 and 4 on either side.) Think about all that as you also consider that there are more than 20 million people in the Mexican capital. And over 4 million cars. Unsurprisingly, commutes often take more than six hours.

2. London

A 2015 survey showed that London commuters are more stressed than in any other European city, that more than 90 percent of them leave extra time to get to work because of frequent delays, and that 49 percent had failed to get to work at all on at least one occasion.* And that's before we start talking about the endlessly miserable weather they have to travel in. Not to mention the extortionate price of their tickets.

1. Beijing

Security checks at many stations mean you have to join lines containing thousands of people even before you get to a platform. The trains themselves are impossibly crowded at rush hour as millions of people hurry to work. Meanwhile, roads leading into the city often experience traffic jams that can last for days. Days!

---

*The research was commissioned by Ford of Europe.

THE TEN MOST EXPENSIVE COMMUTING CITIES IN THE WORLD

The average cost of a one-month ticket on public transport, according to Deutsche Bank's 2017 Mapping the World's Prices survey in US dollars. These prices all add insult to the pain of having to go to work in the first place.

10. Toronto, Canada—$102.7

9. Melbourne, Australia—$105.5

8. Zurich, Switzerland—$106.2

7. Sydney, Australia—$108.4

6. Amsterdam, the Netherlands—$108.6

5. Tokyo, Japan—$110.7

4. New York City, USA—$117.7

3. Auckland, New Zealand—$122.9

2. Dublin, Ireland—$131.6

1. London, UK—$174

THE WORLD'S MOST POLLUTED CITIES

The World Health Organization ranked cities according to annual mean Particulate Matter Concentration between 2008 and 2015. They measured the concentration of fine particulate matter* in micrograms per cubic meter.[†] Anything above 10 micrograms per cubic meter is considered unsafe. Which makes this list another astonishing demonstration of humanity's ability to bite the hand that feeds them.

10. Baoding, China — 126

9. Xingtai, China — 128

8. Bamenda, Cameroon — 132

7. Raipur, India — 144

6. Patna, India — 149

5. Al Jubail, Saudi Arabia — 152

4. Riyadh, Saudi Arabia — 156

3. Allahabad, India — 170

2. Gwalior, India — 176

1. Zabol, Iran — 217

---

*Known as PM 2.5, these are tiny droplets in the air that are less than 2.5 microns in width. There are around 25,000 microns in an inch. They're very small, in other words. But they can do serious damage.
[†] 1 microgram = 0.98 tons; 1 cubic meter = 35.3 feet

THE TEN SADDEST PLACES TO VISIT

Judging by the name, anyway …

10. Futile Lake, Canada

9. Pointless Mountain, Canada

8. Suicide Bridge Road, USA

7. Dead Horse Bay, USA

6. Disappointment Island, New Zealand

5. Misery, France

4. Boring, USA

3. Mount Despair, USA

2. Melancholy Waterhole, Australia

1. Shit, Iran

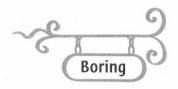

Boring

BRITAIN'S TOP TEN RUDEST STREET NAMES

In 2014, the website needaproperty.com polled 2,000 British adults on the streets they'd be most embarrassed to live on. Ostensibly the survey was carried out to see if the embarrassment had an impact on house value. Apparently, houses on Minge Lane went for £84,000 (over US $100,000) less than on the next street along. Which is interesting. Although really, you can't help suspecting, the survey was done to attract publicity[*]—and because everyone loves a good knob gag.

10. Cock-A-Dobby, Sandhurst, Berkshire

9. Cumming Street, Islington, London

8. Cockshoot Close, Stonesfield, Oxfordshire

7. Cock Lane, Farringdon, London

6. The Knob, King's Sutton, Northamptonshire

5. Crotch Crescent, Marston, Oxfordshire

4. Bell End, Rowley Regis, West Midlands

3. Fanny Hands Lane, Ludford, Lincolnshire

2. Slag Lane, Lowton, Lancashire

1. Minge Lane, Upton-upon-Severn, Worcestershire

---

[*]And I guess if you include appearing in this book as publicity, their scheme worked.

TEN HIGHEST BREXIT VOTES IN THE UK

The results of the British national IQ test held in June 2016, measured by the percentage of voters who voted to leave the EU, by constituency.

10. North East Lincolnshire—69.9 percent

9. East Lindsey—70.7 percent

8. Bolsover—70.8 percent

7. Mansfield—70.9 percent

6. Fenland—71.4 percent

5. Great Yarmouth—71.5 percent

4. Thurrock—72.3 percent

3. Castle Point—72.7 percent

2. South Holland—73.6 percent

1. Boston—75.6 percent

THE TEN NOISIEST CITIES

This Worldwide Hearing Index was developed in 2017 by digital hearing app company Mimi Hearing Technologies, who collated hearing tests of 200,000 of their users, along with data on noise pollution from the World Health Organization and SINTEF (a Norwegian research organization). Alarmingly, the average hearing loss result was discovered to have a 64 percent positive correlation with each city's noise pollution levels.

10. Buenos Aires, Argentina

9. Paris, France

8. Mexico City, Mexico

7. Barcelona, Spain

6. Beijing, China

5. Istanbul, Turkey

4. Mumbai, India

3. Cairo, Egypt

2. Delhi, India

1. Guangzhou, China

CHAPTER 5

FUN AND GAMES

Ancient Roman elites used to talk dismissively of the need to give the people "bread and circuses." The idea was that if the common people were fed and given the distraction of organized games to watch, they wouldn't realize how crappy their lives were and so wouldn't revolt against established power structures. It's amazing how little has really changed in the past 2,000 years, isn't it? The main difference is that instead of getting to watch full-scale re-creations of naval battles and hard-ass gladiators, we're now just left with millionaires kicking balls around. If we're lucky . . .

THE TEN MOST BORING SPECTATOR SPORTS

Watching sports probably isn't as much fun as everyone claims. After all, if it's so great, why do people always drink so much when they're doing it? But still, at least a few beers can make a game of soccer move along. Nothing can help the games on this list.

10. Sailing

9. Golf

8. Ice hockey

7. Golf

6. Quidditch

5. Golf

4. Basketball

3. Golf

2. Football

1. Golf

THE TEN BIGGEST DEFEATS IN MALE INTERNATIONAL SOCCER

Only men this time. It's been depressingly difficult to discover equivalent stats about the female game—which has not received its due of media attention and nerdy stat gathering until quite recently. Hopefully if there's another edition of the book in later years, I'll be able to provide more information about the relevant drubbings. Roll on the day when we can enjoy the embarrassment of female soccer teams as much as the other 50 percent …

8= Yugoslavia 10—Venezuela 0 (1972)

8= Spain 10—Tahiti 0 (2013)

8= Bahrain 10—Indonesia 0 (2014)

8= New Zealand 10—Tahiti 0 (2004)

8= France 10—Azerbaijan 0 (1996)

7. Netherlands 11—San Marino 0 (2012)

6. Spain 12—Malta 1 (1984)

5. Ghana 13—Kenya 2 (1965)

4. Ghana 12—Malawi 0 (1962)

3. Germany 13—San Marino 0 (2006)

2. Brazil 14—Nicaragua 0 (1975)

1. Australia 31—American Samoa 0 (2001)

MOST GOALS CONCEDED BY A PREMIER LEAGUE SOCCER TEAM*

To an extent, this tally represents success. The teams listed have all managed to stay in the top tier for quite a long time, despite conceding lots of goals while they were there. But, then again, Manchester United's tally puts it well outside the top ten. And it's worth publishing this list to finally allow Spurs to come top of something . . .

10. Manchester City—952

9. Arsenal—962

8. Chelsea—963

7. Southampton—1,022

6. Liverpool—1,024

5. Aston Villa—1,186

4. Newcastle United—1,187

3. West Ham United—1,214

2. Everton—1,265

1. Tottenham Hotspur—1,267

*Stats taken on June 24, 2018 from Premierleague.com.

THE TEN WORST THINGS TO DO IN A PUBLIC SWIMMING POOL

Strict rules are necessary when hundreds of nearly naked people gather together in tepid water.

10. Spit

9. Snog

8. Smoke

7. Pick your verruca

6. Pick your scabs

5. Give oral pleasure

4. Receive oral pleasure

3. Masturbate

2. Poo

1. Swim too slowly in the fast lane

THE BIGGEST FAILS AT THE OLYMPICS

Not including doping, corruption, or ridiculous, shameful scandals like allowing the games to take place in Nazi Germany. Or the horrible tragedies like the massacre at Munich in 1972. Those would take up an entire book on their own. And wouldn't be as amusing as the following …

10. Montreal, 1976

Transporting the Olympic flame from Greece to Canada was a big challenge for the organizers of the 1976 Olympics. But they found an ingenious solution. They transmitted an electronic pulse from the flame in Athens via satellite which was used to ignite a torch in Ottawa using a laser beam.* The torch was then carried by hand from Ottawa to the Olympic Stadium in Montreal. Where it rained so much that the flame went out and someone had to relight it using a cigarette lighter.

9. London Olympics, 1908

Italian Dorando Pietri was leading the marathon by a significant margin when he arrived at the stadium during the London Olympics. But he was so tired he became disorientated, started staggering the wrong way around the track, and collapsed. Eventually doctors helped him over the line—still in first place. But then he was disqualified because he'd had help.

---

*Or so they claimed. There's more than a whiff of stink about the whole thing. Which is perhaps why the gods decided to rain on the parade …

8. Munich, 1972

The marathon in Munich in 1972 also had problems. Just before the end of the race, a man wearing a West German track uniform steamed into the stadium and pounded around the track. The crowd cheered in delight. But this man was Norbert Sudhaus, a local student and impostor. Security started chasing him and the crowd began to boo in fury, just as the actual race leader Frank Shorter entered the arena, wondering why the crowd was so angry. "I thought, jeez, I'm an American," Shorter said later. "Give me a break."

7. Sydney, 2000

Cuban taekwondo fighter Angel Matos wasn't happy when a referee retired him after deciding he had spent longer than the allowed minute on an injury timeout. The athlete had a broken toe and it seemed clear he couldn't continue. But he disagreed and went on to prove he still had plenty of fight in him by kicking the poor referee in the face.

6. Montreal, 1976

"The Olympics can no more have a deficit than a man can have a baby," said the mayor of Montreal in the run-up to the 1976 Olympics. But the games were an economic flop. The city ran up $1.5 billion in debt, which took thirty years to repay.

5. Sochi, 2014

Following numerous press complaints about flooding, failing appliances, and the general state of hotels and facilities at the 2014 Sochi Winter Olympics, Russian Deputy Prime Minister

Dmitry Kozak accused the Western media of a sabotage campaign against the hosts and declared: "We have surveillance video from the hotels that shows people turn on the shower, direct the nozzle at the wall, and then leave the room for the whole day." An aide immediately whisked him away before he could give any more inadvertently revealing answers about spy-cams in hotel bathrooms.

4. Rome, 1960

In 1960, the middle-distance runner Wim Esajas was the first athlete from Suriname to qualify for the Olympics. Alas, he failed to turn up for his morning heats. He arrived at the stadium in the afternoon instead, meaning that for years he was dogged by rumors that he had failed to set his alarm clock. Actually there had been a scheduling error and he'd been told the wrong time.

3. Berlin, 1936

At the 1936 Olympics in Berlin, South African boxer Thomas Hamilton Brown was told he had lost his first round lightweight match against Carlos Lillo. He went off to enjoy some really good eating. After all, he'd just spent a lot of time skipping and training and working to a strict diet in order to get into his weight class. Then he was told there had been a mistake, the scores had been switched, and he had actually got through to the next round. He went to the weigh-in, was found to be too heavy, and was immediately disqualified.

2. Rio, 2016

During the first round of the pole vault, Japanese pole vaulter Hiroki Ogita did everything he needed to do to clear the required height. But just as he was clearing the bar, TV cameras appeared to reveal his penis knocking off the bar. Making him an unwilling overnight internet sensation. He originally complained that the media was making up the story to "mock" him. But eventually he watched the video again and said: "This is pretty funny, if I say so myself."

1. Seoul, 1988

Doves were released at the climax of the opening ceremony at the 1988 Seoul Olympics to represent peace and harmony. They were let out right in front of the cauldron containing the flame and so fried on live TV. Which made for a fantastic metaphor, even if it looked alarming to the millions watching.

THE TEN MOST UNFORTUNATE WORLD RECORD ATTEMPTS

You need dedication if you want to be a record breaker. You also need more luck than these unfortunate souls.

10. Amy Hughes

In 2017, Amy Hughes spent seven days running on a treadmill grinding out over 520 miles, only to be told the record didn't count because her boyfriend who was there to witness the challenge couldn't be considered independent.

9. Snapple

Hoping to get some good publicity, the sticky drinks manufacturer Snapple tried to build the world's largest popsicle and sit it upright in New York on a June day in 2005. They brought a 22 ton, 25-foot-long frozen mix by container truck to Union Square and attempted to move it to the upright position using a crane. Ice sculpting specialists were on hand to add the finishing touches. But they hadn't factored in the June heat. The frozen treat immediately started to melt in the sun, sending sugary red juice flooding down the streets, causing pedestrians to flee in alarm and eventually forcing the local fire department to hose down the street.

8. Michel Fournier

Michel Fournier's attempt to freefall from 21 miles above the earth went wrong when the balloon in which he was planning to ascend to the edge of the earth's atmosphere floated away without him. The balloon had cost $500,000. But at least Fournier got in a priceless quip. "This is the first time that something like this has arisen," he said.

7. Californian bubble heads

In 2012, a Californian attempt to get the most people inside a single bubble at one time was ruined when local journalist David Nazar broke the bubble machine.

6. Jesus, glass, pain

On July 12, 2013, a former Cirque du Soleil performer known as Jesus "Half Animal" Villa attempted to record the fastest time flipping through ten panes of tempered glass. He smashed headfirst into the first sheet of glass and broke his neck.

5. Croatian Smurfs

In 2008, 395 Croatians gathered in Split dressed (and face-painted) as Smurfs. They had pictures taken. Took an official count. And sent the details off to Guinness, who let them know that students in Warwick had set a record of 451 Smurfs a year earlier. Somewhere in there, there's an explanation for the current state of the world.

4. Tony Wright

In 2007, Tony Wright made a similar mistake to the Smurf people. He went a grueling 266 hours awake before he allowed himself to collapse in bed, thinking he'd broken the world sleeplessness record by two hours. But some other fool had already managed 276 hours. And, more importantly, Guinness had stopped logging these attempts because they were too dangerous.

3. Hot Kiwis

In New Zealand in 2004, 341 people gathered to walk over a pit of hot coals. And the screamingly obvious happened: twenty-eight people ended up being treated for burns. Looking on the bright side, the event raised over NZ$1,000 for the local fire service. It was just a shame that more than that had to be spent treating the injured.

2. Dutch domino tumblers

In 2005, a Dutch team spent a month arranging 4 million dominoes. Cameras were present to record the breaking of the world toppling record. They instead ended up catching the moment when a sparrow flew into the exhibition center and knocked over 23,000 dominoes. Worse still, the sparrow was then hunted down and killed, prompting threats from animal rights activists. Not least because it turned out to be a house sparrow—an endangered species.

1. Iranian sandwich makers

In 2008, the world's longest sandwich was 507 yards long. An Iranian women's organization drafted in 1,000 people to beat the record, which would require just 6 yards of sandwich per person. They were so confident that they could attain this goal that they let a crowd gather around the production line. The trouble was that it took a long time to put the record-breaking sandwich together and the crowd started eating it before it could be measured.

CHAPTER 6

HEALTH AND WELL-BEING

A balanced diet and healthy living are essential for survival. Which once again makes you wonder how humanity has made it this far.

THE TEN MOST FOOLISH HEALTH FADS

Since the beginning of time, many humans have pursued the body beautiful and the elixir of well-being. And for just as long, charlatans have pursued those poor saps in turn.

10. Charcoal juice

Activated charcoal is useful in the treatment of poisons and drug overdoses because it's very absorbent and stops the bad stuff reaching your internal organs. So why not drink it in juice so that your body doesn't absorb anything from food either? Who needs vitamins anyway? Who cares if it also causes constipation? Who cares if it tastes exactly like what it is—burned wood?

9. Toning shoes

The principle behind these shoes is that they simulate walking over rough ground, and so help you burn extra calories and tone your leg muscles. The reality is that they make no difference at all.[*] But the shoes do sometimes cause leg, hip, and foot pain, thus lessening the amount their wearers walk anywhere—and entirely defeating the objective.

[*] As tested by the University of Wisconsin for the American Council for Exercise, among others.

8. Prancercise

Prancercise has been described by its creator Joanna Rohrback as a "springy, rhythmic way of moving forward, similar to a horse's gait and ideally induced by elation." In other words, you have to try to trot like a horse—and like it. Unlike many of the other fads on this list, prancercise isn't actually bad for you and has similar health benefits to taking a brisk walk. But still. Really.

7. Oxygen bars

In oxygen bars, you can buy oxygen. It's generally bubbled through bottles, then run through a hose inserted into the nostrils and sometimes scented with aroma oils. Aside from providing a useful metaphor for capitalism's ability to charge people for the very air they breathe, there are no proven benefits.

6. Urotherapy

Actually, I can trump that last metaphor. Capitalism can't just trick you into paying for the air you breathe, it can also make money out of you drinking your own piss. In recent years, a mighty stream of health guidance websites have started advocating "urotherapy," citing celebrity adherents and pseudoscience about nutrients and biodynamics. Supposed health benefits include: clearer skin, a cure for psoriasis and athlete's foot, and increased vitality and energy. The actual proven medical benefits include: nothing at all. Oh, and urine isn't sterile. That's a myth. It contains plenty of bacteria.

5. Hawaii chair

The idea behind this motorized chair is that it helps you stay in shape when you're sitting down because a 2,800-rpm "Hula Motor" gyrates your butt around and thus tones your abs. This time the reality is that you can't drink your coffee. And you've just spent loads of cash on something you can do far better with a cheap plastic hoop.

4. Raw water

The ability to provide clean, safe drinking water to all citizens has been a useful measure of human technological progress and an ambition of societies since at least the days of the Romans. The desire to drink "raw" or "live"—unfiltered, untreated, unsterilized, and yes, potentially very dangerous—spring water, meanwhile, is a sure sign of decadence and imminent collapse. Especially since companies have started selling it at almost $40 a bottle.

3. Japanese nightingale-dropping facial mask

What is a Japanese nightingale-dropping facial mask? Why, it's the poo and wee gathered from little birds farmed only on the island of Kyushu! How much does it cost to have this bird-based fecal matter smeared on my face? $220!

2. Colonic irrigation

During this treatment, a rubber tube is shoved into your rectum and then into your colon. Twenty gallons of water and various additives, such as soap or coffee, are pumped in. There are no proven health benefits. There are proven problems, including allergic reactions, infections, and electrolyte imbalances. Plus, it's a plastic tube, going up your ass and hosing your insides. Obviously it's a bad idea.

1. Homeopathy

Homeopaths claim that the things that cause illness can, in tiny doses, be used to help people who are unwell. They repeatedly dilute ever smaller amounts of these substances in water or alcohol in a process called "potentiation," producing an eventual solution so weak that only a "memory" of the original material remains. Or, to use more scientific language: absolutely f*cking none of it. That's right. Homeopathy is the ultimate metaphor for capitalistic endeavor. It makes a huge profit out of absolutely nothing—and often does so at the expense of people who are desperately ill.

THE TEN WORST DIET PLANS

When it comes to letting Weight Watchers down, the following regimens really take the cookie. And the cake.

10. The clay diet

Advocates of this diet recommend stirring bentonite clay into water in order to detox. Doctors point out that eating dirt can bring nasty side-effects, like arsenic poisoning. And that the body detoxes itself naturally anyway.

9. 100 percent raw vegan diet

As our cavemen ancestors first discovered, cooking food is useful for bringing flavor, releasing nutrients, and killing bacteria and other nasties. Going raw only actually makes sense if you want to appear even more self-denyingly pious than all the other irritating vegans on social media.

8. Liquids-only master cleanse diet

Mix apple cider vinegar, cayenne pepper, and maple syrup, and drink that instead of having meals. If you want to go the whole way, celebrity adherents have also recommended drinking laxative tea. So, to recap: that's squirty-poo-tea, vinegar, and burning spice. No amount of maple syrup can make that palatable. And as usual, the health benefits are non-existent.

7. Cabbage soup diet

If you're so happy that you can't bear it, you might want to follow this recipe for guaranteed misery. The cabbage soup diet recommends replacing as many meals as possible with hot fart juice, and ensuring your house smells forever like dogs' bowels. You'll lose your will to live faster than you'll lose weight.

6. Fletcherizing

Toward the end of the nineteenth century, Horace Fletcher became famous for saying that food should be chewed 32 times and then spat out. Or chewed 100 times if you really had to insist on swallowing. He claimed that this method of eating would (radically) decrease the amount of food that people consumed while making them stronger. "Fletcherizing" became a worldwide craze. There were even songs about it.[*] Fletcher himself became a millionaire known as "The Great Masticator."[†] He said: "Nature will castigate those who don't masticate."[‡] Doctors, in turn, castigated him, pointing out that not eating is not healthy.

~~~~~~~~~~~~~~~~~~

[*]Sample lyric:
 "Each morsel you eat, if you'd be wise.
 Don't cause your blood pressure e'er to rise
 By prizing your menu by its size ..."
 (I didn't say the songs were any good ...)
[†]That's Mast*icator*—stop snickering.
[‡]Okay, maybe a little snicker.

146

5. Cigarette diet

"Reach for a Lucky instead of a sweet" advised a series of Lucky Strike adverts in the 1930s. Plenty of other companies also recommended having cigarettes when you felt hungry, pointing to the appetite-suppressing qualities of nicotine. But there were obvious drawbacks.

4. Cotton ball diet

Yes, stuffing yourself with cotton balls when you're hungry is less likely to make you gain weight than eating burgers. But they'll also obstruct your digestive tract, fill your body with toxic dioxins, and leave you starving.

3. The Sleeping Beauty diet

You can't eat if you're asleep. So if you knock yourself out with sedatives, you'll eat less. I suppose there's some logic there—but there are also clear issues for anyone who wants to have a normal life. Still, the diet had its adherents in the latter half of the twentieth century. Elvis Presley was a fan. Yes. That's right. It didn't work.

2. The baby food diet

The idea here is that instead of real food, you should reduce your calorie intake by eating fourteen jars of baby mush a day. But funnily enough, what works for constantly screaming tyrants who weigh less than 22 pounds and have no control of their bowels isn't actually a good prescription for adults.

1. Breatharianism

Breatharians believe that it is possible to live on "light" alone. They say that unpolluted air contains all the nutrients necessary to sustain life and that not eating food will actually increase a person's longevity. One of its most prominent advocates called herself Jasmuheen and claimed she spent six years living on nothing more than herbal tea and the odd chocolate cookie. However, when the Australian TV program *60 Minutes* challenged her to practice what she preached in front of TV cameras, she quickly became ill. Breatharianism received yet more bad press when a journalist sitting next to Jasmuheen on a plane claimed he heard her ordering a meal. And more still when, tragically, several Breatharians died.

THE MOST ABSURDLY EXPENSIVE FOOD

The only thing more sickening than an ostentatiously public display of wealth is eating one.

10. Pizza Royale 007

This pizza contained caviar soaked in Dom Pérignon champagne, lobster marinated in cognac, venison medallions, Scottish smoked salmon, prosciutto and vinegar, and, inevitably, gold flakes. It was sold at a charity auction in Scotland by chef Domenico Crolla in 2006 for $4,200. Probably to a man with a tiny penis.

9. Densuke black watermelon

In 2008, one of these rare watermelons was auctioned off in northern Japan for $6,100. Cheaper than king melons (see number seven). But still crazy.

8. Stilt Fisherman's Indulgence

An Italian cassata* filled with Irish cream, Dom Pérignon, and seasonal fruit attached to a chocolate carving of a stilt fisherman was served up with an 80-carat aquamarine gemstone and put on the menu in the Fortress Resort, Sri Lanka, in 2017. For $14,500. Explain eating that one to the grandchildren.

---

*A kind of sponge cake, often layered with ricotta cheese and candied fruit.

7. Yubari king melons

Only grown in Sapporo, Japan, a pair of these cantaloupes was auctioned in 2008. For $23,500. Meanwhile, I've got some king melons of my own I'd sell for less.

6. Frrrozen Haute Chocolate

In 2007, Serendipity 3 in New York decided their Golden Opulence Sundae ($1,000) wasn't obscene enough and added Frrrozen Haute Chocolate to their menu. It came with a diamond encrusted bracelet, cocoa, milk, gold and whipped cream, and was served up with a gold spoon—all costing $25,000.

5. Fancy taco

A taco containing kobe beef, langoustine, Almas beluga caviar, and black truffle Brie cheese, garnished with a salsa of dried morita chili peppers, civet coffee, and vintage tequila, is served at Grand Velas Los Cabos Resort Mexico, in a restaurant called Frida, for $25,000. Just in case you missed it, here it is again: the restaurant is called "Frida." In honor of the revolutionary socialist artist Frida Kahlo. She'd be so pleased.

4. Golden cannoli

Cannoli are tubular fried pastry shells filled with ricotta cheese. Jasper's of Kansas City, Missouri, wrapped one in gold leaf and sold it (with a diamond) in 2011 for $26,010. Presumably, to a mug.

3. Almas caviar

This Albino caviar is sold in a gold tin for $36,868 per kg. You can get a smaller tin for $1,250. It's just white fish eggs though, so I still wouldn't bother.

2. Chocolate pudding

Four types of Belgian chocolate, champagne jelly, light biscuit joconde, and bitter dark chocolate, glazed with edible gold leaf and topped off with a diamond, sold in 2011 at the Lindeth Howe country house hotel in the Lake District for $35,000. Proof that you can't buy good taste, and nor should you try to eat it.

1. Italian Alba truffle

A 3.3-pound white truffle was sold at auction to a Macau casino owner in 2007 for $330,000. Enough cash to feed maybe a million people.

THE WORLD'S WORST CONCEPT RESTAURANTS

I think we can all agree that the idea of a concept restaurant is inherently bad. Which makes these places all the worse.

10. Buns and Guns, Lebanon

A military-themed restaurant set up in war-torn Beirut in 2008, with sandbags outside, selling dishes with names like "rocket-propelled grenade" and "terrorist bread." After three years of trading it was replaced by a more conventional sport-themed eatery. Its name: Shoot.

9. Hitler's Cross, India

"From small bites to mega joys" said the sign on this Mumbai eatery. It lasted a week in 2006, before the owner, Puneet Sabhlok, realized that the whole thing with ovens and a murderous Fascist wasn't working. "I never wanted to promote Hitler," said Puneet. "I just wanted to promote my restaurant." Stunned after he received hostile media attention, he changed the name and explained he was putting a new culinary rule in force: "no more dictators."

8. S&M Cafes, UK

I know what you're thinking. But the "S&M" in this UK chain doesn't actually stand for that. It stands for "sausage and mash." I know what you're thinking now, too. Stop it. It won't help anyone.

7. Kenny Rogers Roasters, USA

You know, the country musician with the beard. In the early 1990s, there were hundreds of these branded restaurants in the USA, selling fried chicken. They're still popular in Asia. No one knows why.

6. Magic Restroom Cafe, USA

America's first restroom-themed eatery. Also, its last. Customers were expected to sit on toilets and ate signature dishes with names like "golden poop." It opened in 2013—and, drumroll!—it went down the pipes within a year.

5. Cereal Killer Cafe, UK

In 2015, two bearded twin brothers opened a cafe on Brick Lane selling cereal for £2–£5 a bowl. Worse still, they then produced a cookbook featuring delicacies like sausage-stuffed Shredded Wheat. It's this kind of thing that makes people think it's okay to be mean to hipsters.*

4. Cabbages and Condoms, Thailand

I've Googled that combination of words so you don't have to. The good news is that the food is rumored to be excellent and the restaurant raises money to help provide contraception and sexual health schemes in the local community. The bad news is that waiters have been known to wear condoms on their heads. And I'm still not sure what happens with the cabbages.

---

*It's not okay to be mean to hipsters, even so. Many are perfectly nice.

3. Ninja New York, USA

Ninjas are cool, aren't they? But maybe not so much in a restaurant where the guys in dark robes jump out of the shadows, perform magic tricks, or scream at you while you eat. "I began begging for the check just so that I could escape," said a *Time Out* reviewer. In *The New York Times*, Frank Bruni gave Ninja zero stars and predicted that its biggest trick might soon be a "disappearing act." That was in 2005. Bafflingly, it's still open as I write this in mid-2018.

2. Hospitali, Latvia

This restaurant in Riga had staff dressed as nurses who dished up food in hospital-style equipment to patrons sitting in gynecological stirrups, or in strait jackets. It was featured in newspaper articles around the world when it opened in 2009. Even so, a surprisingly small number of people wanted both to think about having doctors poke around their insides and to line their stomachs at the same time. The restaurant was soon taken off life support.

1. Sambo's, USA

When Sam Battinsone and Newell Bonheet founded a restaurant chain in 1957, it maybe seemed like a happy coincidence that their respective first and last names combined to create a massive racial slur. It certainly didn't hold back the expansion of the brand, which had more than 1,000 outlets in the early 1980s. Then everyone woke up and they went bust.

THE TEN WORST VEGETABLES

Let's be honest. Vegetables suck. Especially these ones.

10. Kohlrabi

9. Squash

8. Pumpkin

7. Turnip

6. Red cabbage

5. Cauliflower

4. Sweet potato

3. Brussels sprout

2. Artichoke

1. Jerusalem artichoke

THE MOST DISGUSTING FOODS IN THE WORLD

Proof that there really is no accounting for taste.

10. *Huitlacoche*, Mexico

Huitlacoche means "sleeping excrement." Just in case you need to know more, it's corn infected with a fungus called corn smut, which covers the corn with blue-black spores and cancerous-looking growths.

9. *Bosintang*, Korea

Bosintang's primary ingredient is dog.

8. Crispy tarantulas, Cambodia

Fried venomous spiders. It's said they taste like crab. But I'm certainly not going to try to verify that.

7. *Balut*, Philippines

These are incubated duck eggs. Little feathery fetuses, in other words.

6. *Lutefisk*, Sweden

This is cod soaked in lye: the caustic chemical also used by serial killers to dissolve their victims …

5. *Escamoles*, Mexico

The eggs of a giant venomous black ant. Apparently, they taste buttery. But that doesn't stop them being the eggs of poisonous giant ants.

4. Jellied eels, UK

How do you make an eel even more foul? Chop it up, set it inside a jelly, and serve it up cold with mashed potatoes.

3. Baby mice wine, Korea

As the name implies, this is a drink made up of baby mice, suspended in rice wine. It's said to be a health tonic . . . For the drinker, if not for the mice.

2. *Airag*, Mongolia

As if milking horses wasn't bad enough, someone in Mongolia also decided to ferment the mare juice and use the resulting gloop to get drunk.

1. *Kæstur hákarl*, Iceland

Kæstur hákarl is Icelandic for fermented shark. But that isn't the half of it. The shark in question is the *Somniosus microcephalus* (rough translation: sleepy strangely small head), a cannibal creature that can live for up to 500 years and tends to be overloaded with uric acid and a substance called trimethylamine N-oxide. The former is corrosive wee, the latter can give you heart attacks and make you puke blood. The obvious course of action would be to just avoid this horror fish. Instead, Nordic gourmands like to bury it, let it rot for three months, then hang it out in the air for another few months so it develops a nice crusty layer. It's then dished up with an ice-cold shot of *brennivín*, a fierce Icelandic spirit that dulls the senses (and presumably the intelligence) enough to make the dish bearable.

THE WORLD'S MOST DANGEROUS FOODS

The term "dangerous food" would be almost entirely oxymoronic, if humanity wasn't so reliably moronic. I cannot explain why people eat this stuff.

10. Monkey brains

Monkey brains can cause an illness called Creutzfeldt-Jakob disease, which turns your own brain to mush. Which has a neat circularity considering the state you'd have to be in to eat the things in the first place.

9. Casu marzu

This is a traditional Sardinian sheep's milk cheese infested with cheese fly larvae. These larvae can jump up to 6 in. into the air. They have been known to get into diners' eyes. They can also burn the tongue. Oh, and they can bore through your intestinal walls and make you poo blood.

8. Blood clams

In 1988, blood clams killed thirty-one people in Shanghai, and infected 300,000. If they aren't boiled for long enough, they contain a stew of hepatitis A and E, typhoid, and dysentery bacteria.

7. Alfalfa sprouts

They might be sold to us as a health food, but alfalfa sprouts are ideal breeding grounds for E. coli and salmonella.

6. Cassava

When it's raw, cassava contains a substance called linamarin, which decomposes in the gut to form cyanide. And then kills you. When it's cooked, cassava turns into tapioca pudding. Which is almost as bad.

5. Peanuts

For 99 percent of the population peanuts are delicious, nutritious, and surprisingly nice when made into a paste that sticks to the roof of your mouth. For 1 percent, they are deadly.

4. Ackee

Ackee and codfish is delicious. But unripe ackee, along with the fruit's permanently toxic black seeds, makes people puke so much they die.

3. Hot dogs

Seriously. Children choke on them. In the USA, almost 20 percent of food-related asphyxiations in under-tens are caused by children getting wieners stuck in their throats.

2. *Sannakji* (raw baby octopus)

If you don't chew this Korean delicacy thoroughly enough, its suction caps can grip your throat and choke you. Which might seem like justice, but is still one hell of a way to go.

1. Fugu pufferfish

One fugu* contains enough of a deadly venom called tetrodotoxin to kill thirty people. Symptoms include numbness of the lips, tongue, and fingers; dizziness; slurred speech; headache; nausea; stomach cramps and pain; muscle weakness; and loss of bowel control . . . All followed by death within a few hours, generally from asphyxiation. Meanwhile, although the poison wrecks the body, it doesn't affect the brain. So victims remain fully conscious throughout their ordeal, aware of every second of pain, of the imminence of their death, and of their utter stupidity for trying to eat this fish in the first place.

---

*In western Japan, fugu is known as fuku. And if you cook it wrong, it will.

CHAPTER 7

THE OLDEN DAYS

What happened to the good old days? Where did all the good times go? These questions have always troubled singers and poets, but the answer is pretty obvious. There never were any. History shows us that the best laid schemes of mice and men have nearly always gone awry, and we might as well just embrace it.

THE TEN MOST DISTURBING THEORIES ABOUT CREATION

There are numerous ideas about the origins of the universe, but whichever one you choose, things did not start well for us.

10. The Big Bang theory

In the beginning, there was nothing. But then, something happened. There was a random fluctuation in the void, which we can't quite explain, but which really shook things up. Within a split second, the smaller than subatomic particle that had started things shaking was torn apart by the vacuum around it and our universe exploded into being. It has carried on expanding ever since, although at a slower rate. The edge of the universe is getting ever farther away from us. And we are just one random rock, floating around a random sun, which started dying as soon as it was born.[*]

9. The oscillating model

There is an endless series of Big Bangs in operation and also—oh no!—Big Crunches. Meaning universes are being created and destroyed all the time. Which doesn't bode well for eternity here on earth.

---

[*]Worse still, one of the theoretical end points of this theory is the Big Crunch. Which is as bad as it sounds. In this scenario, the expansion reverses and we all get crushed into nothing again.

8. The eternal inflation theory

This theory is also like the Big Bang—but with an added twist. It posits that the inflation that occurred after the Big Bang never eased off, and that infinite universes are still being created and will continue to be created, also to infinity. Many of these universes may have different physical laws to ours. The possibilities are unendingly mind-bending. For instance, in one potential universe, you have written these words, and I am reading them.

7. The Greek mythological creation myth

The earth and the sky were made out of two halves of a shell from an egg that had been laid by a giant bird with black wings. The egg had also contained Eros, the god of love, who convinced the earth and the sky to get it on and start having children. Those children soon started eating each other, hooking up with each other, and fighting each other. Eventually a god called Zeus triumphed in this war and ordered another immortal called Prometheus to create humans and all the other animals. Prometheus did so—and gave humans fire as a special gift. This enraged Zeus who decided to punish mankind. He sent a box down to a woman called Pandora and filled it with plague, sickness, envy, and greed. He told her not to open it. But she did. And that's why we're so stuffed now.

6. The Chinese Pangu myth

In the beginning, there was nothing. Again. But this time this primordial chaos turned into a cosmic egg. Inside the egg, yin and yang formed—and a hairy giant called Pangu popped into being. He set about separating yin and yang with his giant ax.* They turned into the earth and sky. He started pushing them apart to keep them separated. The earth started growing downward, the sky started growing upward, and Pangu was stretched in between. After 18,000 years of this, he gave up and died. His breath became the wind, his fur bushes and forests, his bones minerals, his left eye the sun, his right eye the moon, and his fleas became animals. So, we're Pangu's fleas.

5. The Rig Veda myth

Purusha had a thousand heads, feet, and eyes. He could wrap his fingers around the world. Which was fine. But the other gods still killed him and turned him into butter. That's right, butter. And this butter was turned into three other gods, the elements, and animals. Which is to say, us. Butter.

4. The Bushongo creation myth

The world was only darkness and emptiness. Then a god called Bumba began to have dreadful stomach pains. Eventually, he began to hurl chunks. First he vomited up the sun, then the moon, earth, plants and animals, and then, just as he was getting to the caustic, bilious stages, humanity.

---

*I'm afraid I don't know where the ax came from. He just seems to have had it. Don't think about that too hard.

3. The biblical creation myth

A bad-tempered god threw the world together in six days. He made us out of clay and decided we should look like him. He took Sunday off to think about it all. Then he sent a snake down to give him an excuse to kick us out of paradise and into eternal punishment.

2. The Ancient Egyptian Heliopolis myth

The god Atum stood on a mound and started masturbating. He—sorry about this—jizzed out the gods Shu and Tefnut. Who were brother and sister, but soon started getting it on, even so. Their children were the sky god Nut and earth goddess Geb. There was a lot more incestuous hooking up and all these various couplings eventually gave birth to everything else.

1. The digital simulation theory

We exist within a computer. We don't know it, but we're just a set of algorithmic formulations. The nice thing about this theory is that it doesn't matter so much that we're making a mess of our ecosystem, because it doesn't exist anyway. The not-so-nice thing is that someone could decide to reboot the computer at any moment. And we've all also got to pray that the thing isn't running on Windows.

THE TEN HARSHEST PUNISHMENTS IN ANCIENT MYTHOLOGY

Those whom the gods loved died young. Those whom they didn't like, meanwhile, had a whole eternity of trouble to look forward to.

10. Lamia

When Hera caught Lamia having an affair with Zeus, the king of the gods' jealous wife stole the younger goddess' children. Lamia went crazy with grief and tore out her own eyes. Then Zeus turned her into a monster with a craving to eat other people's children. Thanks, Zeus!

9. Danaus's Daughters

Danaus had fifty daughters and his twin brother Aegyptus had fifty sons. And if you're thinking "that's convenient," you're thinking just like Aegyptus, who arranged for them all to be married. Danaus wasn't so sure though and told his daughters to kill Aegyptus's sons on their wedding night. Forty-nine of them complied. The gods didn't like that at all and told the murderous daughters that they would now have to wash away their sins in the underworld, using a special basin they were to fill with water from the river Styx. And guess what? The basin leaked and the luckless ladies had to spend the rest of forever filling it up.

8. Io

When Hera found out that Io was having an affair with Zeus, the philandering king of the gods tried to disguise the poor girl as a cow. Hera wasn't fooled and sent a gadfly to repeatedly sting her, driving her crazy and setting her wandering all over the world to avoid its attacks. No doubt lowing like Eric Bana making love in Stephen Spielberg's *Munich*.

7. Marsyas

Marsyas challenged Apollo to a flute-playing contest. Apollo agreed, on condition that the winner could inflict whatever punishment he fancied on the loser. Guess what? Apollo won! Then he had Marsyas skinned alive and turned him into a stream. Which was probably unexpected, but no more pleasant for that.

6. Prometheus

Prometheus was chained to a rock by Zeus because he gave fire to mankind. Every night an eagle came to eat his liver. That must have hurt.

5. Ixion

Because Ixion made a pass at Zeus' wife Hera, the jealous god blasted him with a thunderbolt and then tied him to a constantly revolving wheel of fire. There's definitely a lesson there.

4. Erysichthon

Erysichthon cut down some trees from Demeter's favorite grove to make himself a table. He came to regret this impudence when she cursed him with insatiable hunger. Nothing he ate would satisfy him. Until he finally feasted on his own flesh and died.

3. Sisyphus

Sisyphus was a king who enjoyed killing his own people and those luckless enough to wander into his territory. But he was nothing like as badass as Zeus who rewarded Sisyphus for his life of crime by forcing him to push a boulder up a hill.* With the added refinement that when he got near the top, the boulder rolled back down and he had to start pushing it all over again. For eternity.

*There was also a regrettable incident where Sisyphus annoyed Zeus by revealing Zeus abducted the nymph Aegina. It's very unwise to annoy Zeus.

2. Tantalus

Tantalus was also naughty. He stole ambrosia. And he killed his own son and served him up as dinner to the gods. Bad move. He was chucked into a pool of crystal water in the underworld under a vine of delicious looking grapes. When he tried to eat the grapes they moved away. When he tried to drink the water, it dodged his lips. So he starved for eternity, temptation always just out of reach.

1. Actaeon

When he was out hunting with his dogs, Actaeon saw the goddess Artemis taking a bath. But if he started thinking this was his lucky day, he soon changed his mind. Artemis ordered him not to speak again or she'd turn him into a stag. Naturally, he was unable to obey this command. As he walked off, he instinctively called to his dogs. Instantly he was turned into a stag—and his dogs tore him apart and ate him.

THE TEN CRAZIEST ROMAN EMPERORS

Quite a lot of the information about these emperors comes from pretty unreliable ancient sources. Sometimes they are people whom the emperors had greatly annoyed during their lifetime. Sometimes they're people who lived hundreds of years after the emperors died. But even if these stories need to be taken with a pinch of salt, that doesn't mean they aren't also excellent.

10. Theodosius I (379–395)

Theodosius was a religious extremist. He made Nicene Christianity the state religion even though 90 percent of the population didn't believe in it. He then proceeded to destroy much of the legacy of antiquity, banning the vestal virgins, condemning practitioners of ancient rites to death, allowing the destruction of ancient treasures like the temple of Apollo in Delphi, and—the killjoy—banning the Olympic games.

9. Carinus (283–285)

Ancient sources claim that when Carinus unexpectedly became emperor, he took it as an opportunity to murder everyone who had teased him at school. They also claimed that he had no fewer than nine wives and liked to screw the partners of many of his senators and army officers. This latter proclivity bit him on the ass when one of the officers murdered him.

8. Domitian (81–96)

Early on in his reign, Domitian deified three of his family members—and himself. The self-proclaimed god emperor started out as an efficient administrator, but was as untroubled about killing people as he was by false modesty. Contemporary historians branded him a tyrant whose court was quickly overrun with informers, feeding his paranoia and bloodlust. He punished libel with death—and especially didn't like thespians. He forbade mimes from appearing onstage in public and was also said to have had an actor murdered in the street. Late in his reign he became convinced that he was going to be killed. He became increasingly anxious and fidgety, before going on to be murdered and thereby neatly proving the old adage that being paranoid doesn't mean people aren't out to get you.

7. Caracalla (198–217)

After he killed his brother and sister-in-law, Caracalla made it a capital offense even to mention his brother's name, reinforcing the threat by massacring everyone he suspected of supporting his dead relative. Elsewhere, he did at least have the enlightened idea of offering thousands of people Roman citizenship—but he made things good and weird by stipulating that all the new citizens should call themselves "Marcus Aurelius" after his own first names.

6. Commodus (177–192)

As well as running the usual gamut of murderous egotism and declaring himself a god, Commodus was more than usually obsessed with gladiatorial contests. He often personally entered the arena, killing hundreds of luckless opponents. He also had all the months of the year renamed—after his own twelve (pretty silly) names: Lucius, Aelius, Aurelius, Commodus, Augustus, Herculeus, Romanus, Exsuperatorius, Amazonius, Invictus, Felix, and Pius. Just for good measure, he next had the city of Rome renamed Commodianus.

5. Constantine I (306–337)

Constantine not only inflicted almost 2,000 years' worth of clerical tyranny on the West by promoting Christianity; true to that religion's forgiving precepts, he also poisoned his own son and boiled his wife to death.

4. Tiberius (14–37)

Given what happened to many other emperors, the fact that Tiberius gave up on imperial life in Rome to live in luxurious retreat on the beautiful island of Capri might not seem too silly. Unfortunately, Roman historians claimed that Tiberius spent most of his time there chasing young boys and throwing people off the cliffs.

3. Elagabalus (218–222)

Tragically, Elagabalus wanted ancient physicians to make him a woman—which was medically impossible at the time. He also wasn't cut out for ruling, not least because he came to power aged just fourteen. But that's where sympathy runs out. Alas, Roman historians say he quickly took to murdering children.

He also got caught up in the cult of Elah-Gabal[*] and enjoyed attending rites where human genitals were thrown at monkeys.

2. Nero (54–68)

Tacitus says Nero tried to kill his mother by building a special ship designed to sink while she was in it. When that didn't work, Nero just had her stabbed. He also killed his stepbrother, two wives, and dozens, if not hundreds, of Roman aristocrats. To make things even worse, he was also a keen practitioner of the dread art of performance poetry. He often forced terrified Romans to sit through long recitals of his own verse. Understandably enough, they got fed up with him and had him killed. As the knives went in, he cried: "What an artist dies in me."

1. Caligula (37–41)

The historian Suetonius accused Caligula of sleeping with his sisters, prostituting them, and turning his palace into a brothel. Cassius Dio said that he "consecrated himself to his own service." Which is to say, he became a priest dedicated to worshipping himself. He also appointed his horse as a fellow-priest and demanded that "dainty and expensive birds were sacrificed to him daily." Caligula did at least have the clever idea of invading Britain—but when he got to the Channel, decided it looked too much like hard work. Instead, Dio says, he got his troops to gather up shells and declared that he had just defeated the sea-god Neptune. Soon afterward, his own bodyguards killed him.

---

*A Syrian god from whom the emperor took his nickname.

THE TEN SHORTEST REIGNS OF ENGLISH MONARCHS

Not all English rulers had happy and glorious reigns. Some of them were just nasty, brutish, and short.

10. Harold I (November 12, 1037–March 17, 1040, 856 days)

Confusingly, Harold was also a joint monarch with his (absent) half-brother, Harthacnut, from 1035. But he had himself declared king alone in 1037—and it's from there we measure. This decision in 1037 deeply annoyed Harthacnut, who decided to come over from Denmark and teach Harold a lesson. But just as Harthacnut[*] was planning to invade, Harold died of a mysterious illness[†] at just twenty-four. Harthacnut had his corpse beheaded and thrown into a marsh beside the Thames.

9. Harthacnut (March 17, 1040–June 8, 1042, 813 days)

Harthacnut didn't even last as long as his brother. It's now generally thought he died of a stroke brought on by excessive drinking. The *Anglo-Saxon Chronicle* states that he was

---

*Don't say Harthacnut too quickly.
†The *Anglo-Saxon Chronicle* claims he fell over and "grew black" as he was talking to some monks.

at a wedding and he "died as he stood at his drink, and he suddenly fell to the earth with an awful convulsion, and those who were close by took hold of him, and he spoke no word afterward."

8. Richard III (June 26, 1483–August 22, 1485, 788 days)

Richard was killed by Henry Tudor's army at the Battle of Bosworth Field. His remains were discovered in 2012 in a car park in Leicester.

7. Harold II (January 5, 1066–October 14, 1066, 282 days)

Famously, Harold died with an arrow in his eye at the Battle of Hastings.

6. Edmund II (April 23, 1016–November 30, 1016, 221 days)

Legend has it that Edmund was killed while enjoying a visit to the privy. Some say he was stabbed several times while trying to do a poo. Some say he was shot with a crossbow. It's also possible that he died of wounds following the numerous battles he fought against Danish invaders during his short reign. Or maybe he just died of natural causes. Life was hard in the eleventh century, after all.

5. Matilda (April 7, 1141–November 1, 1141, 208 days)

Bear with me—this is another confusing one. Matilda was also the Empress Maude, widow of the Holy Roman Emperor, and a queen of Germany and Italy. During a period of English history known as The Anarchy,* she briefly gained power from Stephen of Blois—although hostile crowds in London prevented her from actually being crowned. Stephen of Blois reclaimed the throne in November 1141 but Matilda stuck around for quite a few years afterward before fleeing for Normandy. Her son Henry became king in 1154. So, in a way, she had the last laugh.

4. Edward V (April 9, 1483–June 26, 1483, 78 days)

Edward was one of the Princes in the Tower. He reigned briefly under the ironically named "protectorate" of his uncle. This uncle then deposed poor old Edward and took the kingship for himself, as Richard III. Soon afterward, Edward and his younger brother disappeared from the Tower of London. The exact cause of their deaths remains a mystery. Although plenty of people since have hazarded a guess at who might have been to blame …

3. Edgar II (October 15, 1066–December 17, 1066, 63 days)

In a little known footnote to the Battle of Hastings, Edgar was elected king by the surviving Saxon ruling class as a Witenagemot

---

*This was a succession crisis. "Christ and his saints were asleep," according to chroniclers.

council in October 1066. King William had other ideas, however, and Edgar soon found himself paying homage to the Norman conqueror, before being taken into exile. Amazingly, he survived until 1125 and may even have had sons . . . Surprisingly, we haven't heard much from that branch of the royal family since.

2. Sweyn Forkbeard (December 25, 1013–February 3, 1014, 40 days)

Sweyn was king of Denmark from 986. He spent more than a decade raiding, invading, and fighting in England. After a long series of exhausting and bloody encounters, he finally vanquished the opposition and was crowned king. Then he fell off his horse and died. So it goes …

1. Lady Jane Grey (July 10, 1553–July 19, 1553, 9 days)

Also known as the Nine Day Queen, for obvious reasons, Jane's reign was cut short when the privy council that had declared her queen changed its mind and gave the crown to Mary I instead. She survived in the Tower of London until February 1554, when Mary had the former queen executed for treason. Which was a bit rich.

THE TEN WORST POPES

Popes are said to be infallible. But these guys missed the memo.

10. Alexander VI (1482–1503)

Alexander started as he meant to go on, buying the papacy by bribing the electors in a corrupt ballot. He quickly became a byword for nepotism after giving many top jobs to his relatives. He also had a bad habit of killing cardinals so he could inherit their property. Meanwhile, in spite of his vow of chastity, he managed to sire several children and hold legendary orgies in the Vatican. Rumor also had it that he raped his daughter Lucrezia.

9. Benedict IX (1032–1048)

A few years after Benedict's death, his successor Pope Victor III said he had led a "life as a pope so vile, so foul, so execrable, that I shudder to think of it." Victor also accused Benedict of "rapes, murders, and other unspeakable acts of violence and sodomy." Benedict was actually pope on three different occasions. He was expelled from Rome in 1036, but got the Holy Roman Emperor to reinstate him. In 1044, he was again forced out by local opposition to his party lifestyle, but used an army to quell his enemies. Then, confusingly, he abdicated. Another pope was elected, but Benedict decided he liked being pope after all, and came back with an army to reclaim his throne. Finally, another pope was declared and Benedict was excommunicated. It's pretty safe to say that he made a mess of things.

8. John XII (955–964)

The *Catholic Encyclopedia* describes John XII as "a coarse, immoral man, whose life was such that the Lateran was spoken of as a brothel, and the moral corruption in Rome became the subject of general odium." As well as having lots of sex, John XII was fond of murdering people, starting wars, and purging his enemies. He died when he was still in his twenties. The most prominent rumor was that he was killed by a man who found him in bed with his wife.

7. Stephen VI (896–897)

Stephen didn't like his predecessor, Pope Formosus, and he didn't let the fact that Formosus had been dead for six months stop him from enacting revenge when he came to the papacy in 896. Stephen had his enemy exhumed, dressed in robes, and put on trial. To no one's surprise, Formosus was found guilty. Stephen then had several of his fingers removed and his body dragged through Rome and dumped in the Tiber. He was probably prepared to unleash plenty more mayhem, but was himself strangled within his first year in the funny hat.

6. Urban VI (1378–1389)

Urban's election caused a schism in the Church. He found himself facing off several rival popes and beset by enemies on all sides. He did not take a gentle approach. Instead he called for the killing of anyone plotting against him. His reputation became so bad that it was said he complained when the screams of his captives were not loud enough.

5. Boniface VIII (1294–1303)

In 1302, Boniface issued a papal bull declaring that it was "absolutely necessary for salvation that every human creature be subject to the Roman pontiff." He liked power, in other words. He followed up on his words too, waging wars of conquest, destroying numerous cities, and killing thousands of innocents. According to Dante, Boniface also liked to sell indulgences[*]— for which crime the poet said he had a space reserved in the eighth circle of hell.[†]

4. John Paul II (1978–2005)

During John Paul II's reign the priesthood was abusing children on an industrial scale. He oversaw decades of cover-ups. He personally discontinued investigations into prominent abusers. Elsewhere, he also maintained it was a mortal sin to use condoms as AIDS ravaged the world. Several leading African Catholics were even caught telling their followers that condoms had little holes in them through which the HIV virus could penetrate and that they were therefore useless. Unknown millions contracted the virus as a result.

---

[*]An indulgence was an exemption from punishment for a sin, which could be purchased from the Catholic Church.
[†]The murders didn't seem to bother Dante so much. They did things differently in the past …

3. Innocent VIII (1484–1492)

In 1484, the ironically named Innocent issued a papal bull recognizing the existence of witches and urging that such persons be punished "according to their deserts." Over the next two centuries an estimated 500,000 women were killed and unknown hundreds of thousands more were tortured.

2. Pius XI (1922–1939)

In 1930, Pope Pius XI persuaded the German Catholic Center Party to reject cooperation with the Social Democratic Party against the Nazis. Then in 1933, he had the party agree to the Enabling Law, which gave Hitler dictatorial powers. He also signed a friendship treaty, called the Concordat, with the Nazi leader, who said: "The Concordat gave Germany an opportunity and created a sense of trust that was particularly significant in the developing struggle against international Jewry." Elsewhere, in 1936, Pius XI backed the Fascist General Franco in his overthrow of a democratically elected government in Spain.

1. Urban II (1088–1099)

In 1095, Pope Urban II called for a large invasion force to take Jerusalem from the Muslims and the First Crusade began. In the fury that followed, mobs massacred Jews throughout Europe, Orthodox Christians in the East were attacked, and Christian knights rampaged throughout the Middle East. In 1099, the Crusaders took Jerusalem and massacred the Muslim population. We are still suffering the results of his policies. Thanks a bunch, Pope Urban II!

THE WORST US PRESIDENTS IN HISTORY

These presidents are ranked according to the C-SPAN Presidential Historians Survey 2017. A panel of academic advisors were asked by the political cable channel to mark presidents out of ten in ten different categories: public persuasion, crisis leadership, economic management, moral authority, international relations, administrative skills, relations with Congress, vision/setting an agenda, pursuit of equal justice for all, and performance within the context of his times. The top mark went to Abraham Lincoln, who got 906. Donald Trump is yet to be assessed. So it doesn't seem impossible that this list might change in the near future.

10. Martin Van Buren (1837–1841)

Score: 450

Van Buren has been damned by historians for opposing the abolition of slavery and being in power at a time of economic depression. He also helped build the modern Democratic Party. Not everyone sees that as a good thing …

9. Chester A. Arthur (1881–1885)

Score: 446

Mark Twain said that it "would be hard indeed to better President Arthur's administration." For once, posterity disagrees with the great writer. Now the only polls Chester seems to top are about the "most forgotten" presidents. He didn't ruffle many feathers—but it's also hard to point to his big achievements.

8. Herbert Hoover (1929–1933)

Score: 416

Hoover held the reins as the stock market overheated in the summer of 1929—and did nothing to stop it. He presided over the Wall Street Crash that October. Then he opposed federal relief efforts as the world sank into the Great Depression. He flunked it, in short.

7. Millard Fillmore (1850–1853)

Score: 393

Harry S. Truman called Fillmore a "weak, trivial thumb-twaddler who would do nothing to offend anyone"—although, in fact, he annoyed a lot of abolitionists by siding with slavers and enforcing the Fugitive Slave Law.

6. William Henry Harrison (1841)

Score: 383

Harrison died after just 31 days in office, so he can't really be blamed for what followed. But it was still because of him that John Tyler rose to power (see number five). He elsewhere gets black marks because, before his presidency, he played a major role in genocidal wars against Native Americans.

5. John Tyler (1841–1845)

Score: 372

Tyler became the first president to come to power without election, after his predecessor died in office. He also became known as "His Accidency" after he was expelled from his own party, while in office. Another first. But again, nothing to be pleased about.

4. Warren G. Harding (1921–1923)

Score: 360

Harding died of a heart attack while still in office. At the time he croaked, he was actually quite popular with the public. But afterward it became clear he had overseen one of the most corrupt US administrations until the present day. Several members of his cabinet were found guilty of crimes and misdemeanors, and it soon emerged that large-scale bribery scandals had occurred under his watch.

3. Franklin Pierce (1853–1857)

Score: 315

Pierce opposed the abolition of slavery, but, even so, failed to appease secessionist Southern states. He was also a notorious and habitual drunk.

2. Andrew Johnson (1865–1869)

Score: 275

Even with the best will in the world, Abraham Lincoln would have been a hard act to follow. But Johnson went out of his way to make his illustrious predecessor look good. He objected to giving citizenship to former slaves after the Civil War and so helped set in motion the next century or so of inequality and pain in the Southern states. He fell out with Congress to such an extent that efforts at postwar reconstruction were severely hampered, giving a further boost to Southern conservatives. And he was impeached by the House of Representatives.

1. James Buchanan (1857–1861)

Score: 245

Buchanan was another president who failed to address the problems of slavery in the run-up to the Civil War. He also let the issue of secession reach boiling point, so taking the USA to the edge of bloody conflict. And if this list proves anything, it's that American historians are still very annoyed about the Civil War.

THE LEAST POPULAR US PRESIDENTS IN HISTORY

These rankings are based on Gallup polling average approval rates for each president since 1937. For reference, the top ranked president is John F. Kennedy, with an approval average of 70.1. It's also worth noting that these averages are spread out over the presidents' full term of office. So while it's still depressing that Nixon did better than Barack Obama overall, he did become less popular once everyone realized that he was a crook who had bugged the offices of his political opponents and then enacted a gigantic cover-up.

10. Lyndon B. Johnson (1963–1969)

Approval average: 55.1

9. Bill Clinton (1993–2001)

Approval average: 55.1

8. Ronald Reagan (1981–1989)

Approval average: 52.8

7. George W. Bush (2001–2009)

Approval average: 49.4

6. Richard Nixon (1969–1974)

Approval average: 49.1

5. Barack Obama (2009–2017)

Approval average: 47.9

4. Gerald Ford (1974–1977)

Approval average: 47.2

3. Jimmy Carter (1977–1981)

Approval average: 45.5

2. Harry S. Truman (1945–1953)

Approval average: 45.4

1. Donald Trump (2017–)

Approval average: 39.1[*]

---

*As per June 20, 2018. Who knows what will have happened by the time you read this.

THE BIGGEST LIES YOU WERE TOLD AT SCHOOL

Fake news isn't a modern invention. We've been getting plenty wrong for a very long time—and passing it on to our children.

10. Columbus discovered that the world was round

Religious scholars had once objected to the idea that the earth might be round, but by Columbus's time, it was widely accepted as fact. This myth seems to have grown thanks to a fake account[*] written by Washington Irving in the nineteenth century, where the popular author of "Rip Van Winkle" invented an argument between Columbus and a committee in Salamanca. It's actually more likely that people doubted Columbus's plans because he had grossly underestimated the amount of water he would have to cross to get around the world. These objections weren't unfounded—but luckily America was there to stop Columbus and his men from starving to death.

9. Columbus's ships were called the *Niña*, the *Pinta*, and the *Santa Maria*

The *Niña* was really called the *Santa Clara*; the *Santa Maria* was at the time called the *Gallega*. The original name of the *Pinta* is unknown but wasn't *Pinta*.[†]

---

[*]This appears in *The Life and Voyages of Christopher Columbus*.
[†]It's now also thought that Vikings may have reached America long before Columbus. So it goes.

8. Einstein failed his math classes

This story grew up in Einstein's lifetime. He even once encountered a newspaper story headed "Greatest living mathematician failed in mathematics" and put out a correction. In fact, he came top of the class. He mastered subjects like integral calculus* long before his peers. He taught himself algebra and came up with his own proof of Pythagorean theory. So sadly you can't console yourself with this one if your children can't calculate.

7. Van Gogh cut off his own ear

It's now thought Paul Gauguin cut off the ear with a sword during a drunken fight, and that once Van Gogh and his friend had sobered up they quite understandably decided to keep quiet about what had happened.

6. George Washington cut down his father's cherry tree

The story is that young George chopped down the tree with a little ax he'd been given for his sixth birthday. When his annoyed father asked what happened, he said: "I cannot tell a lie . . . I did cut it with my hatchet." But ironically enough, the whole thing was a fabrication, made up in 1806 in the fifth edition of

*A famously complicated branch of math related to the areas between and under curves and the accumulation of quantities. Don't worry if you don't know what that means. Pretty much no one did until Isaac Newton perfected the theory.

a biography of the great man written by a bookseller glorying in the name of Mason Locke Weems.

5. Your tongue has different taste regions

For decades, children used to be shown a "tongue map," illustrating a tongue with a region for sweet tastes, another for salty, and two bits up the edge for sour. But all parts of our tongues detect all tastes.

4. Humans only use 10 percent of their brains

Sadly, we use just about all the gray matter we've got. So we don't have latent extra potential to unlock. And, yes, I know what you're thinking. This fact definitely rules out the possibility of telepathy.

3. Kilts are Scottish

The ancient Highlands garment was introduced to Scotland by an Englishman, in the eighteenth century. Thomas Rawlinson had noticed that the actual Highland dress* worn by his employees north of the border was "a cumbrous unwieldy habit" so he got the tailor from the local (English) army regiment to design something more suitable. The tailor came up with the kilt design and the rest is history—but maybe not history as Scottish nationalist kilt wearers would prefer it.†

---

*Which was much more like a modern full dress than a kilt.

†Clan tartans are an even later invention than kilts. They were also invented by Englishmen. Oh, and until the nineteenth century, the traditional instrument of the Highlands was the harp rather than the bagpipes.

2. Blood is blue in the body

The story we used to be told is that blood turns red with exposure to oxygen in the air. This ignores the fact that we'd actually be in quite a bit of trouble if there was no oxygen inside our bodies. And that blood is always red.[*]

1. Chameleons change color for camouflage

In fact, it's generally the opposite. Chameleons change color when they want to communicate with other chameleons. Generally to let them know how angry or horny they are feeling. Sometimes they will change in order to help regulate their temperature, going dark if they want to absorb heat and pale if they want to reflect it.[†]

---

[*]Veins look blue thanks to the fact that red light is less good at penetrating skin than blue light—so we see the blue more clearly.
[†]Boy George fans! The good news is that these facts make no difference to the essential meaning of the lyrics of "Karma Chameleon." You could even argue that an interesting new layer is added because the chameleon's color change can be motivated by sex …

THE TEN MOST ABSURD BUT ONCE POPULAR SCIENTIFIC THEORIES

One of the definitions of a good scientific theory is that it has to be testable, and it has to be possible to prove it wrong. So maybe these foolish ideas show that science works. Maybe.

10. Resonance causes bridge collapse

In 1831, a bridge in Lancashire collapsed while a regiment of soldiers crossed it in lockstep. Fortunately, the bridge went over a shallow bit of river and no one died. Unfortunately, everyone got it into their heads that the soldiers' marching had caused a resonant frequency that brought the bridge down. Ever since, soldiers have been ordered to break step while crossing bridges. Even though it was later discovered that the bridge that fell down in 1831 had faulty bolts. And that that kind of resonance can't bust bridges at all.

9. Phrenology

This was the idea that you can measure intelligence and personality through the shape of bumps on the head. The theory was so prominent in the nineteenth and early twentieth centuries that companies used it when interviewing job candidates. Sherlock Holmes stories were based upon it, and criminal defendants were convicted if "expert" phrenological witnesses decided they didn't like the way their heads were shaped. Later scientists proved conclusively that head bumps have nothing to do with intelligence at all. Oh well. At least the people with pointy heads got to the truth eventually . . .

8. The miasma theory

Until Pasteur proved the existence of germs, it was thought bad smells, rotten air, and even dirty thoughts caused disease. They didn't.

7. Subliminal messaging

The notion that images briefly flashed up on screens might convince us to drink Coca-Cola, eat popcorn, vote right wing, worship Satan, or engage in other forms of depravity is frightening—but also complete balls. The idea was hugely popular in the 1960s, with organizations like the CIA running their own mind-control programs. But it was all the invention of a market researcher called James Vicary who came up with it as a wheeze to advertize his failing consultancy. The experiments he claimed to have run in order to prove his theory were bogus. He eventually admitted the whole thing was a gimmick, but by then it was too late. If only he'd set out to prove that people will believe any old nonsense . . .

6. Rats caused plague in the seventeenth century

It would be nice to be able to blame rats for spreading this catastrophic disease, if only to confirm our prejudices against these icky animals. But most of the available evidence suggests that the great plagues of the 1660s moved too fast to be spread by rats. Plus there's the fact that when people fled from London to the countryside they took the plague with them—but not the rats. It's also notable that the disease eventually decimated Iceland—even though there were no rats there at the time.

5. Hysteria

The idea that imbalance in the womb drove women crazy was popular from the time of the Ancient Greeks. It took on an extra dimension in the sixteenth century when a Dutch doctor suggested genital stimulation might cure the (nonexistent) problem. By the nineteenth century, doctors were regularly trying to give their female patients health-giving paroxysms by hand. This practice was apparently quite tiring—so doctors began to invent mechanical agitators, and eventually vibrators.[*]

4. Eugenics

The notion that only the fittest should be allowed to breed and that, for instance, laziness could be hereditary became hugely popular at the start of the twentieth century. It was especially popular among right-wingers and Nazis for obvious and chilling reasons—but it was also prevalent on the left. The Campaign for Nuclear Disarmament peace campaigner and otherwise widely respected brainiac Bertrand Russell once proposed everyone should be given color-coded "procreation tickets" according to their breeding potential and that those who had children with the wrong ticket-holder should be fined. Which doesn't sound very romantic. Anyway, alongside the moral problems this theory creates, it also turns out to be a great way of wiping out genetic diversity and thus weakening humanity: the exact opposite of its intentions.

---

[*]So in the end, they did actually make life better for some women, even if unintentionally.

3. Alchemy

From the fifteenth century to the start of the nineteenth, a great deal of scientific endeavor was devoted to attempting to convert base metals into gold. Leaving aside the fact that no one ever managed to carry out the conversion (because it is impossible), this idea was especially stupid because if anyone had found a way to make limitless gold, the no-longer-rare metal would consequently have become worthless.

2. Maternal impression

For most of humanity's existence a basic scientific principle seems to have been: if in doubt, blame women. This pernicious theory suggested that if pregnant women had bad thoughts, or were frightened or moved by some other emotional stimulus, that would have an impact on their unborn fetuses and cause birth defects or later psychological issues.

1. Tobacco is good for you

Soon after explorers brought tobacco back from South America, people began to believe that a good smoky enema could cure everything from constipation to epilepsy. Smoke was also often directed up the rectums of people who fell in rivers—as if drowning wasn't already problem enough. The practice continued until the early nineteenth century—by which time it was beginning to be understood that tobacco was actually a toxin—and "blowing smoke up your ass" became another way of saying that someone was flattering you with nonsense.

THE WORST MEDICAL PROCEDURES IN HISTORY

It's amazing that medicine has developed into a skilled and knowledgeable profession. Because for most of history it's been practiced by quacks, charlatans, and accidental killers ...

10. Trepanning

An ancient treatment whereby a hole is drilled into the skull to relieve pressure on the brain and let out bad spirits. I don't think I need to explain why this doesn't work.

9. Lobotomies

By the mid-twentieth century, doctors took things one step further than trepanning and started removing whole sections of the brain in order to relieve various psychiatric symptoms. Unfortunately, lobotomies also severely impaired other mental functions. And—here's a surprise—they were mainly carried out on women and minority groups. The originator of the procedure won a Nobel Prize. Its advocates claimed that it made the custodial care of patients far easier. Critics noted that killing them would produce the same results.

8. Dead mice

In Elizabethan England, doctors recommended cutting a mouse in half and applying it to warts to get rid of the offending outcrops. Again, I think you can see for yourself why this might not be a good idea.

7. Soothing syrups

One nineteenth- and early twentieth-century solution to the perennial problem of wakeful, noisy toddlers was to feed them "soothing syrups." But there were, as a 1910 *The New York Times* article explained, problems: "An investigation . . . has revealed that morphine sulphate, chloroform, morphin hydrochorid, codein, heroin, powdered opium, cannabis indica, and combinations of these dangerous "soothers" supply the active ingredient in nearly all the soothing syrups sold." With all this special extra juice in them, the syrups did a good job of keeping troublesome tots quiet. But also quite often killed them.

6. Amphetamine-based diet pills

On the plus side, putting speed into diet pills often did make 1950s women lose weight. It also, many of those women noticed, helped with the drudgery of housework. Unfortunately, speed use often made people psychotic, gave them heart problems, and was accompanied by long, slow, depressing comedowns.

5. Tapeworm-based diet pills

Not only is this an entirely disgusting idea, it may well have been a hoax. Manufacturers in the 1920s claimed to sell pills containing real tapeworm eggs and dehydrated worms, but most were fakes.

4. Mercury

In early modern Europe, mercury was used to cure syphilis and constipation. It didn't work. But it did cause heart attacks and lung problems, tremors, chest pains, muscle spasms, depression, and suicidal tendencies. Mozart was just one of the thousands of victims of mercury poisoning.

3. Bloodletting

From Greek times until the nineteenth century, popular medical theory held that four humors governed the body and its ability to fight illness: black bile (melanchole), yellow bile (chole), phlegm, and blood (sanguinis). Too much black bile and you're melancholic; too much yellow bile and you're choleric; too much phlegm and you're phlegmatic; too much blood and you're sanguine. Oh, and you need to be drained . . . Unknown thousands were therefore killed by doctors letting blood from them with unsterile instruments when they were already weakened by illness.

2. Hemiglossectomy as a method to combat stammering

In this procedure, half of the tongue was cut off. With no anesthetic. It didn't work. Unless you count being unable to say anything and/or being dead a reasonable remedy.

1. The goat gonad cure

In Kansas in the 1920s, a fake doctor called John Romulus Brinkley made a fortune from inserting goat gonads into men and women in order to cure impotence and other sexual problems. He made so much money and became so popular that he was nearly elected governor of the state. Unfortunately, he was also responsible for the death of unknown hundreds and possibly even thousands of people and is now thought to have been one of the twentieth century's most prolific (if accidental) killers.

CHAPTER 8

MODERN LIFE

Every generation loves to claim that times are getting harder, our morals are slipping, and our customs are becoming ever stranger. Every generation tends to be wrong. In spite of everything, humans have done some things right. It's better to live now than at almost any other time. Life expectancy has been steadily increasing, violent crime has been decreasing, food is fresher and nicer, even TV is producing more and more masterpieces, like the third season of *Twin Peaks*. But that doesn't mean that there aren't still challenges out there. And that we don't consistently fail to meet them.

THE DUMBEST TRENDS ON YOUTUBE

10. The banana challenge

Can you eat a banana while wearing tights over your head? Obviously not. But that hasn't stopped thousands of people from trying—and continuing to do so long after the joke grew old. It turns out that if you've seen one person stuffing a banana through tights, you've seen them all. But thousands of the films got made even so.

9. The banana and Sprite challenge

Not to be confused with the banana challenge—beyond the fact that it's also very silly. This time the idea is to eat two bananas and down a liter of Sprite without vomiting. Since the stomach can't hold all that Sprite anyway, it's chunks ahoy. It's like we're living through a discount version of the last days of the Roman Empire.

8. The Kylie Jenner challenge

Some people liked Kylie Jenner's lippy pout and so decided to get one of their own by sticking their lips in a shot glass and sucking until they got bruised and swollen. This became a craze and spawned hundreds of thousands of videos. It also spawned plenty of glasses shattering and people getting shards stuck in their faces.

7. The cold water challenge

Jump in an icy lake. Swim to shore, if you don't die. As did several luckless people who attempted this challenge back in 2014.

6. The salt and ice challenge

The theory is that if you put salt on your skin, then ice, it will be extra hurty because salt lowers the freezing point of water. The theory was proved correct in thousands of videos. Alas, it also scarred and burned the skin of participants, many of them children.

5. The cinnamon challenge

Participants must swallow a spoonful of ground cinnamon in one minute. Without water. Thus coating their mouth and throat, inducing gagging, vomiting, and hilarity. Also, the inhalation of powder into the lungs, emphysema, lung scarring, and the odd collapsed lung. Between January and March 2012 (when the challenge was getting 70,000 mentions a day on Twitter), the American Association of Poison Control Centers took 120 emergency calls related to the gag that quickly turned into gagging up your guts.

4. The condom challenge

Put a condom in your nostril, snort it into your throat and pull it out of your mouth. If this works according to plan, it's disgusting and painful. If it doesn't, you risk getting an item designed to withstand a good pounding stuck in your windpipe—and then you die.

3. The choking game

Get a friend to cut off your air supply by pressing on your chest. Or putting you in a choke hold. Or hell, just do it yourself with a noose. Even those that this trend doesn't kill end up suffering because brain cells don't grow back after they've been deprived of air. I know. I know. The joke writes itself.

2. Neknomination

Drink a load of alcohol very quickly on camera, and challenge two friends to do the same. Someone upped the ante by making specially toxic cocktails. Someone else drank water with a goldfish in it. Someone else, gin with a dead mouse in it. During the peak of the trend in 2014, at least five people died from alcohol poisoning in London alone.

1. The fire challenge

People record themselves being covered in flammable liquid, and then setting themselves on fire. At the time of writing there are over 65,000 related videos on YouTube. If you need me to point out the likely problems, you're probably in the right market to make an addition to the canon.

THE TEN STUPIDEST KITCHEN GADGETS

Some people help build spaceships. Some invent energy saving devices that will help us ward off global warming. And some spend their time coming up with things you don't need in the kitchen.

10. Max Space Butter Mill

You load your butter into a canister, put on a top with a twisty handle, twist the twisty handle, and then the Max Space Butter Mill dispenses a thin strip of butter: thus doing exactly what you could have done using a knife, and your brain.

9. Creative Kitchenware Egg Yolker

A device that separates egg yolks from egg whites using suction. Yes, that's right, it sucks. It's also another solution for a problem that doesn't exist. It looks far harder to use this than it is to just separate the egg parts by swapping them between the two halves of the broken shell.

8. Prepworks by Progressive Tuna Press

What is a Prepworks by Progressive Tuna Press? It's a straining device that helps you drain the oil or brine from your can of tuna. You put it on top of the opened can, press it down, upend the can and squeeze out the juices. What does the Prepworks by Progressive Tuna Press do that you can't just do with the opened lid of the can? Once again, nothing.

7. Chef'n Peel'n Onion Peeler

People have managed to peel onions for thousands of years using a knife and their hands. This device does nothing extra. For $17.

6. Sylvania omelet maker

An expensive electric device containing a small housing in which you put your omelet ingredients before closing the lid, turning on the power and, yes, you guessed it, doing what everyone else can do just as easily in a pan.

5. Oster Electric Wine Bottle Opener

At last, a device on this list that can do something the normal contents of most kitchen drawers can't do far better. Unlike a corkscrew, the electric wine bottle opener can run out of charge and thus help keep you sober.

4. Fondoodler

A hot cheese hose. You load cheese into a cartridge. It heats up. You squeeze it out in hot worms. I don't know why.

3. Bacon Express bacon cooker

This is like a toaster for bacon. Do I need to go on? Okay. It costs $40. You hang the bacon over a heating element, like greasy underwear on a radiator, close the device up, set a timer and then wait, your bacon hidden from view and dripping fat into a receptacle. As your favorite snack inevitably overcooks, you can only hope that, one day, someone will invent something better. For instance, a kind of open flat metal plate with a handle you can use on your stove top instead ...

2. Egg cuber

Allows you to make cube-shaped hard-boiled eggs. Which makes you wonder if eggs are the wrong shape in their natural state. Then realize that they aren't.

1. Ham Dogger*

A tubed device into which you cram meat and other ingredients in order to make a hot-dog shaped hamburger. Because life is already futile enough, so why not also shape your beef into a vaguely turdish symbol for the uselessness of everything?

*It really is called a Ham Dogger. I'm afraid I'm not making any of this stuff up. As of May 24, 2018, you can find it online here: http://www.kitchenart. com/ProductDetails.asp?ProductCode=18550

THE TEN MOST DANGEROUS HOUSEHOLD OBJECTS*

More accidents happen at home than anywhere else. They are also often more embarrassing than any other accident.

10. Extension cords

Not only do they cause thousands of fires every year, they also trip up another few thousand people and send them to the ER.

9. Lawnmowers

Just think about it.

8. Hot tubs

When they aren't busy drowning people and giving them cardiac arrests, hot tubs breed bacteria.

7. Bleach

You'd think people would know drinking it is unhealthy by now. But still it takes out hundreds of people every year. It can also cause serious inhalation injuries and burns.

*This list is based on information from the US Consumer Product Safety Commission, Occupational Safety and Health Administration, and the National Fire Prevention Agency.

6. Swimming pools

They're nice. But they also account for 350 deaths a year in the US alone.

5. Candles

They too are nice. But they still cause almost 5 percent of all home fires.

4. Televisions

The bigger they get, the more they hurt when they fall on you. And they injure more than 40,000 people a year in the USA.

3. Power tools

Power tools are responsible for almost half a million visits to emergency rooms in the USA every year, for reasons that don't need explaining.

2. Trampolines

These cause an astonishing 100,000 injuries annually in the USA alone. Who'd have thought that a device that sends people flying into the air could be so dangerous?

1. Stairs

Yes, they are useful. But they still kill more than 10,000 people in the USA every year.

THE TEN MOST HARMFUL DRUGS

A 2007 study in the *Lancet* led by David Nutt, the UK chairman of the Advisory Council on the Misuse of Drugs, asked UK experts in psychiatry, pharmacology, and addiction to rate drugs according to three types of harm: physical health effects, potential for dependence, and social harms. The study was called "Development of a rational scale to assess the harm of drugs of potential misuse." The word "rational" was a not-so-covert dig at the UK government's drug policy, which then (as now) treated drugs like Ecstasy, LSD, and cannabis as much more dangerous than many legal substances that did far more harm. Anyway, each drug was then given a score out of three and ranked accordingly.

10. Buprenorphine — 1.6

An opiate used for pain control.

9. Tobacco — 1.54

An addictive stimulant leaf that is dried, rolled up, and smoked to give people the illusion that they are 1950s French film stars.

8. Amphetamine — 1.6

A psychostimulant that combats fatigue, suppresses hunger, and gives people a weird liking for furiously high beats-per-minute techno from Germany.

7. Benzodiazepines — 1.62

A hypnotic relaxant used to combat insomnia and anxiety. Includes drugs like diazepam and temazepam. Shaun Ryder of the Happy Mondays developed a liking for them. Which might explain why the most famous review of their fourth album *Yes Please* read simply: "No thanks."

6. Ketamine — 1.68

A mild hallucinogen, popularly known as a horse tranquilizer, but used more often as an anesthetic for cats. Which doesn't sound quite as cool.

5. Alcohol — 1.71

A psychoactive substance used to make going to parties more endurable and as a shield against the weather in northern countries.

4. Street methadone — 1.9

A synthetic opioid used as a substitute treatment for heroin addicts.

3. Barbiturates — 2.2

Synthetic sedatives that are used as anesthetics.

2. Cocaine — 2.3

A stimulant made from the coca leaf. Renowned for its ability to make boring people talk even faster and more insistently about their worthless lives. Almost certainly a contributing factor to the 2008 financial crash. And especially addictive when smoked as crack.

1. Heroin — 2.7

A derivative of the opium poppy originally used as a painkiller that quickly became more simply a killer. It is fiercely addictive and unless properly administered presents a high risk of overdose and enjoying bebop jazz.

THE MOST EXPENSIVE DIVORCES IN HISTORY

More proof that love hurts. Determined by the size of the settlement in dollars.[*]

10. Robert L. Johnson from Sheila Johnson, 2014— $400 million

Robert Johnson, who cofounded the network Black Entertainment Television with his wife Sheila, was the first African American billionaire. Not long after she was awarded $400 million, Sheila married the judge who presided over the case. Funny that.

9. Mel Gibson and Robyn Moore Gibson, 2006— $425 million

The largest Hollywood payout to date. It represented half of Mel Gibson's fortune at the time.

8. Craig McCaw and Wendy McCaw, 1997— $460 million

Mobile phone pioneer Craig and newspaper publisher Wendy remained friends after the divorce, but Wendy walked away with a fortune in stock in a company called Nextel. Alas, a

---

*Correct as of June 15, 2018.

telecommunications share meltdown wiped much of the value from the shares two years later.

7. Dmitry Rybolovlev and Elena Rybolovlev, 2014 — $604 million

Elena was initially awarded $4.5 billion after complaining about her Russian oligarch husband's infidelities. Although the $604 million she was finally given remains quite a tidy sum.

6. Adnan Khashoggi and Soraya Khashoggi, 1980 — $874 million

That's around $2 billion in today's money. Adnan made his fortune dealing arms in Saudi Arabia. So it's hard to feel too sorry for him.

5. Harold Hamm and Sue Ann Arnall, 2012 — $974.8 million

Sue Ann Arnall, wife of the oil magnate, initially held out for more and didn't deposit her check until 2015.

4. Steve Wynn and Elaine Wynn, 2010 — $1 billion

This was actually the second time the casino billionaires had been married to each other. They also divorced in 1986. Lawyers will no doubt be hoping that they marry again.

3. Bernie Ecclestone and Slavica Radić 2009 — $1.2 billion

When this divorce was announced, it was widely assumed that the Formula 1 magnate had made one of the biggest payments in history to his wife of twenty-four years. But it later emerged she was actually paying him a tasty $100 million a year from a trust fund he had transferred to her name. Things are different on Planet Rich.

2. Rupert Murdoch and Anna Murdoch, 1999 — $1.7 billion

Seventeen days after making this payout to his wife of thirty-one years, the evil billionaire tyrant married Wendi Deng.

1. Alec Wildenstein and Jocelyn Wildenstein, 1999 — $3.8 billion

Alec and Jocelyn split up after she walked in on him in her bedroom with a Russian model and he threatened her with a gun. During proceedings, the judge prevented her from using alimony to have expensive cosmetic surgery procedures, but still awarded her $100 million a year for thirteen years in addition to a one-off payment of $2.5 billion.

THE WORST CAR TO BUY DURING YOUR MIDLIFE CRISIS

You've wasted your life. You haven't seen your friends for years. Your favorite jeans no longer fit around your expanding waist. Your hearing's going. Your doctor has told you that you drink too much. It's sad. But buying a car that goes nought-to-sixty in less than ten seconds won't necessarily help.

10. Porsche 911

Instead of spending $112,000, why not just get a badge that tells everyone that you can no longer get an erection.

9. Ford Sierra Cosworth

When Julius Caesar reached his forties, he wept because he hadn't yet achieved as much as Alexander the Great. Now men just buy cars that were popular during their childhood. Caesar went on to conquer Gaul. But you, alas, will not be able to turn the clock back.

8. Dodge Viper

Sure, it's fast—but everyone will know the only reason you're really going to need that kind of horsepower is that your bladder isn't as reliable as it used to be, and you never know quite when you're going to get caught short.

7. Jeep Wrangler

World War II nostalgia is a dreadful thing. It gave us Brexit and it gives us people chugging through streets where children play in cars designed to break through Nazi fortifications. It might make you feel like General Eisenhower, but you'll just look like Sergeant Bilko.

6. Ford Mustang

Owning this muscle car will unleash your inner James Dean— and if you aren't careful, send it flying straight through a windscreen.

5. VW camper van

In spite of its hippy-dream heritage and the promise of sleeping by the beach, this surprisingly expensive purchase will quickly degenerate into an excuse to cluck over crockery, do extra packing, indulge in advance planning, and obsess over hookup points.*

4. Bentley Continental

People like to say that when you buy a Bentley you get what you pay for. And it's true. You get an overpriced car.

---

*No, not that kind. The ones you use to plug in your TV because you're having another night alone inside your van.

3. Audi TT

The fact that you're over forty doesn't give you a license to refuse to use turn signals at roundabouts. Nor does it mean you're allowed to overtake on blind corners. You may be feeling all too close to death, but please don't use a car that doesn't even have room for shopping to endanger the rest of us.

2. Range Rover

They say "laughable," you hear "successful." They say "environmental desecration," you hear "envy." They say "please stop blocking the roads outside our schools," you hear Coldplay pumpin' on your very expensive stereo. They are right.

1. BMW 5 series

Nothing says "wanker" quite like a BMW.

THE TEN WORST CARS OF ALL TIME

As listed in the annual *Auto Express* readers' poll from September 2017. *Auto Express* is British, so it's possible there's a slight bias in this list toward the clunkers the UK used to put out in the 1970s. But then again, no one made awful cars quite as well as we did.

10. Vauxhall Frontera

An SUV hybrid as ugly as its name. Not so much the final frontier as the last time anyone bought anything from Vauxhall.

9. FSO Polonez

A car from the Eastern Bloc when it meant something. The nadir of Communist manufacturing in a weird hatchback body.

8. Reliant Robin

A three-wheeler remembered affectionately by anyone who watched Del Boy driving one in the TV comedy *Only Fools and Horses*. But not so affectionately by anyone who remembers actually driving one.

7. Morris Marina

Next time a Leave voter tells you things were better before the UK joined the EU, give them this abomination to drive.

6. Rover CityRover

A super mini without any super. The last car MG Rover produced in the early 2000s gave the impression that the main reason the company was going under was because everyone had given up.

5. Alfa Romeo Arna

A cross between an Alfa Romeo and a Nissan, but not in a good way. Had the styling of Nissan at their worst and the kind of unreliability and electronic mayhem that only Alfa could provide.

4. SSangYong Rodius

A Korean people carrier with a strange boxy extension on the boot that made it look like a hearse—only without the joie de vivre.

3. Chrysler PT Cruiser Convertible

The roofless version of a car already considered one of the ugliest of all time. The joke was that now you could see the face of the poor person driving it.

2. Austin Allegro

The nadir of British manufacturing in the 1970s. Which is saying something. Ugly, unreliable, uncomfortable, overpriced, and featuring a weird square steering wheel.

1. REVA G-Wiz

An electric car built in India. Original models had a range of less 50 fifty miles, a power output of 13kW (less than plenty of starter motors) and leaky roofs and windows. They also had next-to-no crumple zones, were notoriously dangerous, and barely moved if you tried to squeeze more than one person inside.

THE TEN WORST COMPUTER GAME RELEASES OF ALL TIME ACCORDING TO METACRITIC*

Metacritic, the website that aggregates scores for reviews, also covers computer games. To qualify, the games have to have received seven or more reviews. And be really, really bad.

10. Infestation Survivor Stories (The War Z) (2012)

Platform: PC

Score: 20

Concept: A post-apocalyptic nightmare. Ninety-five percent of the human race has been wiped out. You have to scavenge and fight zombies to survive, while all the time this dire game zaps your actual will to live.

Sample review: "If you see this game approach you, do not panic. Simply aim for the head, attempt a decapitation or set it on fire." INC Gamers

*http://www.metacritic.com/browse/games/score/metascore/all/all/filtered?sort=desc&page=152—as accessed on May 18, 2018. All scores are out of 100. The Legend of Zelda: Ocarina of Time on the N64 came top with 99.

9. Deal or No Deal (2007)

Platform: Nintendo DS

Score: 20

Concept: The Noel Edmonds TV program transferred to a computer game. There are 26 briefcases containing different amounts of money. You want to open the case with the most money in it. Except it really doesn't matter, because it's a computer game and there's no money. Which makes it another good metaphor for life. But horrible to play.

Sample review: "Save yourself the trouble and just say 'No Deal.'" Gamers' Temple

8. Alone in the Dark: Illumination (2015)

Platform: PC

Score: 19

Concept: It's dark. There are monsters that are allergic to light. So you run around trying to provide illumination and then kill the monsters.

Sample review: "Fall for its misleading charms and you really will be taught the true meaning of horror." *Metro*

7. SPOGS Racing (2008)

Platform: Wii

Score: 18

Concept: You race a thing that's shaped like a wheel with a disk in the center, containing a picture of a crash helmet facing toward you, rather than the track ahead. This "spog" is based on a once faddish toy to which the game developers didn't have the rights. It rolls very slowly around a track that looks like an escapee from a badly pixelated 1980s game. There are other spogs rolling slowly around it too. And an unrelated soundtrack of revving noises. And that's about it.

Sample review: "There's more fun to be had in reading instruction manuals for toasters." *Nintendo Gamer*

6. Double Dragon II: Wander of the Dragons (2013)

Platform: XBox 360

Score: 17

Concept: A remake of a popular 1980s game. You get to be a character called Billy or Jimmy and kick people.

Sample review: "So terrible that its existence is nothing short of a miracle." Hardcore Gamer

5. Vroom in the Night Sky (2017)

Platform: Switch

Score: 17

Concept: You get to ride a magic bike and collect stardust. You are called Magical Luna Girl. You need to open a magic gate. The more stardust you get, the more powerful your magic bike becomes and if you don't care after simply reading this nonsense, imagine how you'd feel after playing it.

Sample review: "An absolute travesty of an experience that should never have been allowed onto the eShop in the first place." Pocket Gamer UK

4. Leisure Suit Larry: Box Office Bust (2009)

Platform: PlayStation 3

Score: 17

Concept: You have to complete a series of pointless challenges in a Hollywood movie studio setting while your character swears and complains about how pointless the challenges are. In a boring way. There's also crappy porn and horrible jokes about women.

Sample review: "With a process as complicated as game development, there's the potential for a lot of things to go wrong. With Box Office Bust, what went wrong turns out to be almost everything." IGN.com

3. Yaris (2007)

Platform: XBox 360

Score: 16

Concept: A free game. You get to ride around in a Yaris car pimped up with weapons in a transparent (but failed) attempt to make you want to buy a real life hunk of junk from Toyota.

Sample review: "Unfortunately, there are actually no redeeming qualities to Yaris." GamesRadar+

2. Ride to Hell: Retribution (2013)

Platform: PC

Score: 16

Concept: You're a biker in the 1960s. You ride a bike that can only go forward. You also have to shoot people and be offensive to women, and have awkward fully clothed sex with those women.

Sample review: "Stay clear of this game as if it was a puddle of oil on the highway." *CD Action*

1. Family Party: 30 Great Games Obstacle Arcade (2012)

Platform: Wii U

Score: 11

Concept: Thirty minigames in one. That sounds like a bargain—until you look at the games. One involves rolling dice from a cup. The highest score wins. And that's it. It would bore Ancient Romans, let alone digital natives.

Sample review: "I'm really upset that it isn't illegal to sell garbage like this to innocent children." Eurogamer, Sweden

CHAPTER 9

THE FUTURE

The Danish cartoonist Robert Storm Petersen once said: "It's hard to make predictions—especially about the future." But that hasn't stopped people from trying. And failing. Predictably enough.

THE TEN MOST WAYWARD PREDICTIONS ABOUT COMPUTER TECHNOLOGY

Experts don't deserve their bad reputation. They get far more things right than they get credit for. But it's still funnier when they get things wrong …

10. *"Everyone's always asking me when Apple will come out with a cell phone. My answer is, 'Probably never.' "*

David Pogue, *The New York Times* in September 2006 (the actual answer was June 2007).

9. *"The idea of a wireless personal communicator in every pocket is a pipe dream driven by greed."*

Andy Grove, then CEO of the Intel Corporation, speaking to *The New York Times* in 1992. Perhaps not coincidentally, Intel missed out on plenty of the lucrative smartphone action in years to come.

8. *"We don't need you. You haven't gone through college yet."*

A Hewlett Packard executive wasn't interested in Steve Jobs and Steve Wozniak's "personal computer" invention in 1976—so the pair went off and founded Apple.

7. *"I think there is a world market for maybe five computers."*

Thomas Watson, chairman of IBM, 1943.

6. *"Remote shopping, while entirely feasible, will flop—because women like to get out of the house, like to handle the merchandise, like to be able to change their minds."*

Time Magazine, February 1966

5. *"Nicholas Negroponte, director of the MIT Media Lab, predicts that we'll soon buy books and newspapers straight over the internet. Uh, sure. So how come my local mall does more business in an afternoon than the entire internet handles in a month?"*

Clifford Stoll, the distinguished scientific teacher, author, and astronomer, was asking the wrong question in *Newsweek* in 1995.

4. *"Apple [is] a chaotic mess without a strategic vision and certainly no future."*

Time magazine, February 1996.

3. *"Apple's erratic performance has given it the reputation on Wall Street of a stock a long-term investor would probably avoid."*

Fortune, February 1996.

2. *"I predict the internet will soon go spectacularly supernova and in 1996 catastrophically collapse."*

Robert Metcalfe, founder of 3Com and inventor of Ethernet, writing in a 1995 *InfoWorld* column. In 1999, Metcalfe put a copy of this column into a blender, mixed it up, and ate it.

1. *"Two years from now, spam will be solved."*

Bill Gates, at the World Economic Forum in 2006. By 2012, it accounted for 90 percent of all email.

THE TEN MOST WAYWARD PREDICTIONS ABOUT CINEMA AND TELEVISION

As these quotes show, a hard landing awaits anyone who tries to foretell what's going to happen on our screens outside the remit of the programming schedule.

10. *"Cinemas will have disappeared [by 1984] because it requires less effort to view the same kind of pictures on the television screen."*

Critic Sir Herbert Read saw television conquering all in the *New Scientist* in 1964.

9. *"TV will die in a decade."*

Critic Mark Ravenhill was less certain about victory when writing for *The Guardian* just over a decade ago, in November 2007.

8. *"My invention . . . can be exploited for a certain time as a scientific curiosity, but apart from that it has no commercial value whatsoever."*

Auguste Lumière, the French co-inventor of the Lumière motion picture camera, speaking in 1895.

7. *"Talking films are a very interesting invention, but I do not believe that they will remain long in fashion."*

Louis-Jean Lumière showed he was just as prescient as his brother Auguste when quoted in *Films* in 1928.

6. *"The cinema is little more than a fad. It's canned drama. What audiences really want to see is flesh and blood on the stage."*

Charlie Chaplin was confident about his future career prospects in 1918.

5. *"Moving pictures need sound as much as Beethoven symphonies need lyrics."*

Charlie Chaplin got it wrong again in 1928.

4. *"The talking motion picture will not supplant the regular silent motion picture."*

Thomas Edison might have invented a talking picture machine in 1913, but he couldn't see it going anywhere.

3. *"We do not want now and we never shall want the human voice with our films."*

D. W. Griffith gives readers of *Colliers* magazine his view of the future in 1924.*

---

*Given that he directed the racist Civil War epic *The Birth of a Nation*, his view of the future is at least more welcome than his view of the past.

2. *"Who the hell wants to hear actors talk?"*

Harry M. Warner (president of Warner Bros Pictures) was still asking the wrong question when he was shown a prototype Vitaphone sound film system in 1925.

1. *"Colour and stereoscopy will make cinema into the greatest art in the world. Bad films will be impossible."*

John Betjeman was feeling optimistic in 1935.*

---

*In his defense, he was speaking a good fifty years before *Police Academy V* came out.

THE TEN MOST WAYWARD LITERARY PREDICTIONS

Writing is often characterized as the battle against oblivion, the fight for immortality, the only thing that counts. Authors who stand the test of time have reached the highest pinnacle of their trade. But pity their critics. They are generally remembered only when they get things spectacularly wrong. Just as they do in these mistaken auguries.

10. *"An oxymoronic combination of the tough and tender,* Of Mice and Men *will appeal to sentimental cynics, cynical sentimentalists . . . Readers less easily thrown off their trolley will still prefer Hans Andersen."*

Time magazine on John Steinbeck's *Of Mice and Men* in 1937. The novel still sells thousands of copies in the USA and UK every year, and remains a fixture on exam set text lists.

9. *"Little imagination is shown in invention, in the creating of character and plot, or in the delineation of passion . . . M. de Balzac's place in French literature will be neither considerable nor high."*

A critic called Eugène Pitou confidently puts Honoré de Balzac in his place in the *Revue des deux mondes* in 1856. Turned out, Balzac's place remains higher than Pitou's.

8. *"We cannot name one considerable poem of his that is likely to remain upon the threshing-floor of fame ..."*

The *London Weekly Review* passes judgment on Samuel Taylor Coleridge, author of *The Rime of the Ancient Mariner,* in 1828.

7. *"It is not to be accepted easily, it cannot be read in a half dose, and by the great public which multiplies editions it may remain neglected or unknown."*

The Manchester Guardian warns its audience about Joseph Conrad's *Lord Jim* in 1900.

6. *"The final blow-up of what was once a remarkable, if minor, talent."*

The *New Yorker* reviews *Absalom, Absalom!* by William Faulkner in 1936. Nine years later, he won the Nobel Prize.

5. *"What has never been alive cannot very well go on living. So this is a book of the season only ..."*

The *New York Herald Tribune* on *The Great Gatsby* by F. Scott Fitzgerald in 1925.

4. *"There are two equally serious reasons why it isn't worth any adult reader's attention. The first is that it is dull, dull, dull in a pretentious, florid and archly fatuous fashion. The second is that it is repulsive ... Mr Nabokov ... failed."*

The New York Times advised readers not to read Nabokov's *Lolita* in 1958. Readers decided otherwise.

3. *"A hundred years from now it is very likely that 'The Jumping Frog' alone will be remembered."*

Harry Thurston Peck makes a prediction about the works of Mark Twain, the author of *Huckleberry Finn*, in the *Bookman* in 1901.

2. *"In* Wuthering Heights *. . . all the faults of* Jane Eyre *are magnified a thousandfold, and the only consolation which we have in reflecting upon it is that it will never be generally read."*

James Lorimer warns readers of the *North British Review* not to expect much of Emily Brontë in August 1849.

1. *"His fame is gone out like a candle in a snuff and his memory will always stink."*

William Winstanley underestimates John Milton—and neatly contradicts himself by including him in his *Lives of the Most Famous English Poets* in 1687.

THE TEN MOST WAYWARD
PREDICTIONS ABOUT GEOPOLITICS

War! What is it good for? Making powerful men look stupid.*

10. *"The coming of the wireless era will make war impossible, because it will make war ridiculous."*

Guglielmo Marconi, radio pioneer, *Technical World Magazine*, October 1912

9. *"George, you're crazier than hell."*

John F. Kennedy berates his Undersecretary of State George Bell for suggesting in 1961 that the decision to send troops to Vietnam could lead to escalation of the war there.

8. *"Victory is in sight."*

General Paul D. Harkins was optimistic about the prospects in Vietnam in 1963. The war dragged on until 1975—and the USA lost.

7. *"There can be no doubt as to the verdict of future generations on his achievement. He is the greatest figure of*

---

*It's always men. Meanwhile, although Edwin Starr claimed that war was good for "absolutely nothing," it's generally proved quite useful for arms manufacturers and oil magnates.

our age. Mussolini . . . will dominate the twentieth century as Napoleon dominated the early nineteenth."

Lord Rothermere writes in the *Daily Mail* in March 1928.

6. *"Among the most difficult problems of the world, the Arab–Israeli conflict is one of the simplest and most manageable."*

Walter Lippman, respected columnist, April 17, 1948.

5. *"The War That Will End War."*

H. G. Wells on the First World War in August 1914.

4. *"We're going to hang out the washing on the Siegfried Line."*

Song written by Jimmy Kennedy for the British Expeditionary Force in 1939. The Siegfried Line was a chain of fortifications across Germany's western border. The BEF never got near the line. Instead it was evacuated from Dunkirk in May 1940.

3. *"In the victory of the immortal ideas of Communism we see the future of our country."*

State Anthem of the Soviet Union, 1977 version. The hammer and sickle flag was lowered for the last time from the Kremlin on December 25, 1991.

2. *"Mission Accomplished."*

A backdrop behind George W. Bush as he gave a speech about the Iraq war on board USS *Abraham Lincoln* on May 1, 2003. The war lasted until 2011 and ended with the country divided and the creation of the Islamic State. Nice work, W.

1. *"My good friends, for the second time in our history, a British prime minister has returned from Germany bringing peace with honour. I believe it is peace for our time. We thank you from the bottom of our hearts. Go home and get a nice quiet sleep."*

British Prime Minister Neville Chamberlain on September 30, 1938, after concluding the Munich Agreement. War broke out one year later.

THE TEN MOST WAYWARD PREDICTIONS ABOUT ECONOMICS

When economists and politicians tell you things can only get better, you just know it's going to get worse.

10. *"Stocks have reached what looks like a permanently high plateau."*

Professor Irving Fischer, Yale economist, 1929, one week before the Wall Street Crash and the start of the Great Depression.

9. *"Let me speak . . . head on. There will be no recession in the United States of America."*

President Richard Nixon, January 30, 1974. By July it was confirmed that the economy had entered recession.

8. *"We feel that fundamentally Wall Street is sound and that for people who can afford to pay for them outright, good stocks are cheap at these prices."*

Goodbye and Company, market letter to customers, quoted by *The New York Times*, October 25, 1929.

7. *"There are going to be no devaluations, no leaving the European Exchange Rate Mechanism. We are absolutely committed to the ERM. It is at the centre of our policy.*

We are going to maintain sterling's parity and we will do whatever is necessary, and I hope there is no doubt about that at all."

Norman Lamont, August 26, 1992. Twenty days later, Britain left the ERM.

6. *"As the rate of technological change in computing slows, the number of jobs for IT specialists will decelerate, then actually turn down; ten years from now, the phrase information economy will sound silly."*

Paul Krugman, Nobel Laureate economist, 1988.

5. *"[The impact of] problems in the subprime market seems likely to be contained."*

Federal Reserve Chairman Ben Bernanke in Congressional testimony on Capitol Hill on March 28, 2007. Just over one year later the subprime mortgage crisis went global.

4. *"At present, my baseline outlook involves a period of sluggish growth, followed by a somewhat stronger pace of growth starting later this year …"*

Federal Reserve Chairman Ben Bernanke (again), this time on February 14, 2008, in congressional testimony on Capitol Hill. Lehman Brothers crashed in September. The world economy enjoyed ten years of recession and stagnation.

3. *"The Soviet economy is proof that, contrary to what many skeptics had earlier believed, a socialist command economy can function and even thrive."*

Paul Samuelson, the first American to win the Nobel Prize in economics, speaking in 1961.

2. *"We can have confidence in the long-term foundation of our economy . . . I think the system basically is sound. I truly do."*

George W. Bush, July 15, 2008.

1. *"There is no cause to worry. The high tide of prosperity will continue."*

Andrew W. Mellon, Secretary of the Treasury, September 1929, on the eve of the Great Depression.

THE TEN MOST WAYWARD
PREDICTIONS ABOUT DOOMSDAY

The end is never quite as nigh as the prophets say.

10. Predicted end of world: February 1, 1524

Astrologers in London predicted that the end of the world would begin with a huge deluge of rain on February 1, 1524. Twenty thousand people left their homes. The Prior of St Bartholemew's built a fortress where he set himself up with enough food for two months. The skies remained dry.

9. Predicted end of world: 1806

In 1806 in Leeds, a hen began to lay eggs carved with the words "Christ is Coming." Naturally, hundreds of people traveled to see the miraculous fowl and began planning for the approaching End Times. They were disappointed when it was soon afterward discovered that Mary Bateman, the owner of the chicken, had been fetching the message into the eggs with a mild acid and then—I'm sorry to tell you—reinserting them into the poor bird to lay again.

8. Predicted end of world: 1999

A hundred and fifty Taiwanese people dressed in white clothes and wearing cowboy hats suddenly arrived in Garland, Texas, early in 1998. It was Chen Tao—or True Way—a group led by the charismatic Ho-Ming Chen. They had just bought more than thirty properties and they claimed that they had a spaceship. This Godplane was capable of holding 100,000 people and was going to lift the repentant out of trouble when Armageddon came in 1999. Excitingly, God was due to broadcast details about the unfolding End Times on Channel 18 of the local TV network at midnight on March 25. When the appointed time for this miraculous broadcast arrived, Chen and his followers were surprised to find that the cable network wasn't running any programs at all. All that they could see on the screen was snow. The "God program" had been due to run until March 31, at which point God was going to come and shake hands with everybody in the world and speak to them in their own language. When this didn't happen either, Chen held a press conference and admitted: "Since God's appearance has not been realized, you can take what we have preached as nonsense."

7. Predicted end of world: 2000

Shortly before the millennium, the former rockabilly singer Buffalo Bill Hawkins managed to convince some 3,000 people that he was a "witness" who would announce Christ's second coming. Next, he would be murdered by Satan and usher in the end of the world. All of this would happen before the end of the year 2000. He and his followers (many of whom had also changed their name to Hawkins) hid out in an armed compound in scrublands near Abilene, Texas. "Thankfully, we only have a year left of this madness," said Hawkins in 1999. By the end of the following year, it was clear he was wrong.

6. Predicted end of world: Unspecified

Joanna Southcott was an author and prophet who drew huge crowds to her talks in the early nineteenth century. She died tragically. Although aged sixty-five, she had told her many followers she was pregnant with the Messiah—but the growth in her stomach turned out to be cancer. Those disciples took some solace, however, because she left them a large sealed box, which she had promised contained the prophecy of the end of the world, as foretold in the Gospel of St John, and the secret to eternal bliss. This box came with the instructions that it wasn't to be opened until a time of great crisis—and then only in the presence of no fewer than 24 bishops of the Church of England. That didn't stop the antiquarian researcher Harry Price from taking a look in 1927, however, when he staged a public opening. He and the onlookers were surprised to find that the contents included a horse pistol, a lottery ticket, a dice box, a purse, some old books, and a nightcap.

5. Predicted end of world: 1200–1260

In late twelfth-century Italy, a mystic called Joachim of Fiore emerged from a long session of "wrestling" with the book of Revelation and proclaimed that he'd uncovered a hidden message. He'd learned that the Third Age would begin sometime between 1200 and 1260, when everyone would be able to start enjoying the good times of peace and harmony. By the end of 1260, the final catastrophe hadn't occurred and his remaining followers began to grow annoyed. They had been told that beating themselves with iron spikes would hasten the glorious day on. It hadn't. Instead, hundreds of people ended up sore and sorry.

4. Predicted end of world: AD 440–500

Around AD 440, a man calling himself Moses of Crete claimed the apocalypse was going to strike in the fifth century AD— and he should know because he was the Messiah. He claimed to have been sent from heaven to lead his followers back to the Promised Land. And he would prove his powers by making the sea part and leading them through it, just like his namesake in the Bible. He gathered hundreds of people, took them to a precipice by the sea, told them the waves were about to part, and ordered them into the waves. Dozens of people obeyed him. But the sea didn't. Those who weren't drowned were killed on the rocks below. Moses himself was never heard from again. It's unknown whether he too perished or simply fled.

3. Predicted end of world: December 31, 2012

December 2012 marked the end of the Great Cycle of the Maya Long Count Calendar after 5,125 years. Plenty of people thought that the world would go with it. Not least because a planet called Nibiru was hurtling toward us. NASA's website received thousands of questions in the run-up. Some people asked if they should be worried. Some if they should kill themselves and their pets. A man in China even built himself a giant Noah's ark in preparation. Luckily he didn't need it. The calendar didn't end—it just began another long cycle. The planet Nibiru didn't actually exist either.

2. Predicted end of world: March 21, 1843–March 21, 1844

William Miller was a charismatic prophet who managed to convince 50,000 followers that the world would end between March 21, 1843 and March 21, 1844. Many of these followers abandoned their homes. None voted in elections—because why bother? Those who were farmers refused to plant their crops. Some of them even began to climb up trees and onto the top of buildings so they could be the first to see the descent of Jesus and be ready to float into heaven. In several towns, local wags took to letting off trumpet peals. Millerites mistook these for the first announcements of Christ's imminent arrival and jumped off their perches in order to fly up and meet Him. The results were predictably painful. On March 22, Miller became the subject of considerable scorn in the popular press. But many followers stuck with Miller. "I still believe the time is not far off!" he said hopefully, and soon hit upon a new day to pray for: October 22, 1844. On the morning of the appointed day, thousands and thousands* gathered on hilltops and the roofs of high buildings, arms outstretched, as they waited for The Rapture. In the afternoon they were still there. By the evening they were fatigued. On the morning of October 23, they were depressed. There followed a mass nervous breakdown among the traumatized Millerites. The non-event went down in history as "The Great Disappointment."

---

*Some estimates put the figure as high as one in every seventeen residents of the US at the time.

1. Predicted end of world: 1914, 1919, 1921, 1926, 1941, 1955, 1976, and, erm, "soon"

The Watchtower Tract and Bible Society of New York (aka the Jehovah's Witnesses) was proven wrong in its prediction that the world would end in 1914. On the first days of January 1919, 1921, 1926, 1941, 1955, and 1976, similar predictions were equally conclusively refuted. New Year 1926 was an especially disappointing year for the Witnesses because in the build-up they had invested an awful lot of money in a California mansion where they intended to house the Old Testament prophets Abraham, Moses, David, and Samuel, whom they thought had been due to return to earth in 1925. Nowadays they just restrict themselves to saying "the end will come" without specifying when.

CHAPTER 10

THE END

Ultimately, it sounds like we're in trouble.

THE TEN MOST LIKELY WAYS THE EARTH IS GOING TO END

The world might just end with a bang rather than a whimper, after all.

10. Volcano eruption

In 1783, an eruption in Iceland lowered the average annual temperature in the USA by 9 degrees. And that was nothing. Sixty-five million years ago, there began a centuries' long eruption of magma in India that released a quarter-of-a-million cubic miles of lava. Some scientists think it was this eruption that helped finish off the dinosaurs. Before that, some 250 million years ago, a Siberian volcano is thought to have caused the largest extinction on record. And true, that was a long time ago. But there's currently a super-volcano bubbling away under Yellowstone. And scientists have no idea when it's going to blast off.

9. Solar flares

Sometimes stars like our sun can brighten briefly. One of the theories is that it's because of powerful magnetic outbursts known as coronal mass ejections, or superflares. But no one really knows why. However, that's not the issue. The issue is that it does happen. And if our sun started behaving in this way, the earth would be fried within a couple of hours.

8. Asteroid impact

Massive lumps of space rock smashing into earth at terrifying speeds. You can understand why this scenario has people worried. And even if the impact doesn't take out entire continents, it could still cause firestorms, acid rain, and dust clouds that would land us in a perpetual winter. The good news: according to data compiled by *The Economist* in 2013, the odds of an asteroid destroying the earth are 1 in 74,817,414. The bad news: ten years ago, you'd have got longer odds on Donald Trump becoming president. That didn't work out well either.

7. Comet impact

Uh oh! Asteroids have evil cousins. Whereas asteroids are made of rock and metal, comets are made of ice and dust. Which sounds like Megadeth compared to Simon and Garfunkel. Except, comets can be 6 miles in diameter and can travel at around 100,000 mph. Which is likely to hurt.

6. Sun bloat

In about 7 billion years, the sun is going to turn into a red giant. Our star will grow so big that the earth will find itself inside it. It's hard to think of a way that might be good for us.

5. Biotechnology

As well as the risk of genetically engineered plants having unforeseen and catastrophic effects on ecosystems, we now have the potential to mass-produce biological pathogens that could quickly wipe out entire populations and make the film *Twelve Monkeys* look like an episode of *My Little Pony*.

4. Terminators

It's quite possible that Artificial Intelligence will soon become smarter than humans. At which point, the robots may well begin questioning what use we are, and whether we are worth all the trouble. Even if robots don't become self-aware, their algorithms may still lead them to do destructive things. Right now, there are robots in existence that can find their own power sources and independently use weapons systems. And Arnie isn't getting any younger …

3. Global epidemics

It's quite a long time since the Black Death wiped out a quarter of Europe's population, but since then AIDS and the 1918–1920 Spanish flu epidemic have shown what disease can do by taking over 20 million lives each. We've also been working hard to speed up global travel and thus ensure that diseases can move faster than ever and reach all corners of the earth, while simultaneously overusing antibiotics, creating evermore resistant strains of diseases like cholera and measles.

2. Nuclear war

The USA and Russia alone have almost 19,000 active nuclear warheads. At the time of writing, they are respectively led by a racist rapey clown and a psychopathic KGB hardman with compensation issues.

1. Global warming

We are already experiencing glacier retreat, changes in the timing of seasonal events, and declines in Antarctic sea ice. And the more the earth warms up, the worse it gets. Water evaporation, for instance, pumps water vapor into the atmosphere, which is itself a greenhouse gas, and so traps more heat, which could drive carbon dioxide from the rocks . . . and on it goes. If we don't drown, we'll fry. Or starve. And the worst thing about it will be that it will be our fault. Just like everything else. (Except maybe the bullet ants. Even we can't be blamed for those little bastards.)

NOW YOU COME UP WITH
YOUR OWN 10 WORST
OF EVERYTHINGS ...

THE 10 WORST ....

10.

9.

8.

7.

6.

5.

4.

3.

2.

1.

THE 10 WORST ....

10.

9.

8.

7.

6.

5.

4.

3.

2.

1.

THE 10 WORST ....

10.

9.

8.

7.

6.

5.

4.

3.

2.

1.

THE 10 WORST ....

10.

9.

8.

7.

6.

5.

4.

3.

2.

1.